COMMITTED BY CHOICE

Religious Life Today

Judith A. Merkle

A Liturgical Press Book

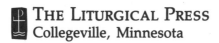
THE LITURGICAL PRESS
Collegeville, Minnesota

1   2   3   4   5   6   7   8   9

Library of Congress Cataloging-in-Publication Data

Merkle, Judith A.
    Committed by choice / Judith A. Merkle.
      p.   cm.
    ISBN 0-8146-2072-8
    1. Monastic and religious life. I. Title.
    BX2435.M44 1992
    255—dc20   92-23588
                                                 CIP

To my parents,
Kathleen and Charles Merkle,
in honor of their
fiftieth anniversary of marriage,
with love and gratitude

Contents

IV. CURRENT ISSUES IN RELIGIOUS LIFE

Preface

We face a critical dilemma today: how to explain what religious life is, its grounding, and its future in a time when each of these topics, once taken for granted, is now being questioned. This book was written in response to this challenge. To it, I bring the voice of some of the new theologies since the council, which bring a contemporary adult faith experience in the Church to an understanding of religious life. This is done in order to rearticulate its basic grounding. The development of these chapters did not arise out of an interest in whether religious life has a future (because the author believes it has) but more out of concern for the direction of that future.

Three main ideas are developed in these pages. To be a religious today means to come to terms with a culture which has little room for a life commitment based on religious inspiration and concern with global human development. It is a choice to be committed. To grow as a religious means to move through a stage of healing and need for personalization in communities since Vatican II, toward a deeper sense of mission, community, and generative action in the Church and society. Finally, to talk about religious life today, we need a new language, one that speaks to adults who are conscious of their capacity to direct their own lives and the world around them. This means that we must examine the basic language used to talk about religious life to see if it is adequate to reflect the contemporary adult experience of being called to this distinctive type of discipleship.

This writing is not a treatise on vows. It discusses the vows, but it asks more foundational questions, since the questions surrounding religious life today are basic. Do the vows exist? Is religious life a distinctive vocation in the Church, or is the religious vocation an illusion, having no uniqueness? Religious life is considered in these pages as an adult stance in the Church, a categorical choice—that is, a choice that eliminates other choices. In that sense, like marriage, it presupposes the assumption of certain life directions and the laying aside of others. It is a path of conversion.

Other questions also arise today: why be a member of a religious congregation? I can work in the Church without this framework. What is the mission of my congregation now that many of the institutional commitments it once held are gone? How is a religious community different from a group of professionals who share a living space? Is religious life a therapeutic life style concerned with healing of hurts or does it meet a need in the Church and the world? What should we be doing to pass on our charism to the next generation?

This book explores these questions by developing four main concerns.

Part I examines the nature of the choice to be a religious today in light of conflicting images of success and autonomy in our society. It discusses the countercultural nature of religious commitment as a sign, among others, of a vocation to religious life.

Part II looks at the period of transition in which religious congregations find themselves after thirty years of renewal efforts and asks the question, what are the next steps? What resources have we gained to move forward? It explores the challenge in recent literature to move beyond the liberal model of religious life into a new paradigm of self-understanding and mission.

Part III examines the meaning of the vows. Are they a path to heaven or to a new earth? How do we combine in our language of the vows the basic religious experience which grounds them and the commitment to the poor, the Church, and global justice which they inspire?

Part IV treats current issues in religious life today: the future of community life, its relationship to the Church, and the new partnerships being formed through the reorganization of religious congregations and through new forms of association today. It poses the question, what will the religious community of the future look like?

Since this text is primarily on religious life, I have often used such terms as "vocational commitment" and "the life of the vows" to refer to that vocation. I have done this knowing that religious life is only one calling that can lay claim to these terms. Also, this writing speaks specifically to active religious congregations, although many of their concerns are shared by men and women religious in contemplative orders. Written primarily for religious and their friends, those people considering religious life, and men and women in new partnerships with religious congregations as associates and lay volunteers, it will also be of interest to those living the commitment of priesthood today as we share common concerns about a vocation which is a commitment by choice based on a religious experience.

Many of the questions addressed in this book have arisen in conversations I have had not only with the members of my own community but many others. Some of these reflections began as talks given in my province, the Ohio Province of the Sisters of Notre Dame de Namur and then shared with others. The response of sisters in my community, those of other communities, and friends encouraged me to continue to explore these questions in book form. Also, the sections of this text on commitment have been discussed often with newer members in religious communities and the students and faculty at The Athenaeum of Ohio/Mt. St. Mary Seminary in Cincinnati. These reflections incorporate some of their experience of what it means to opt for a life commitment in the Church today.

I owe many people thanks for help in preparing this text, especially Elizabeth Bowyer S.N.D.deN. for reading the text in its various drafts and for sharing her friendship and encouragement. I wish also to thank Mary Ann Barnhorn S.N.D.deN., our provincial, for her support and interest in its development; Srs. Marla Feldman and Marie Morris for providing a space to work during our general chapter so I could complete this text; Marilyn Kerber, Agnes Havlik, and Susan Youst, the members of my local Notre Dame community, for our many winter-evening chats on its contents; Pat Brockman O.S.U. for her companionship; Roger Haight S.J. for sharing his love of theology; and my aunt, Ann Merkle C.PP.S., for her good example and support through the years.

International friendships and exposure have deeply shaped this text. I owe much to conversations with Margaret Madden of the Sisters of Mercy of Brisbane, Australia; Pia Buxton I.V.B.M. of

London, England; the Sisters at Loretto College, Toronto, Canada; John Veltri S.J. of Loyola House, Guelph, Ontario; the Sisters of Good Shepherd and the Jesuits at the Loyola House of Studies, Ateneo de Manila, the Philippines; and the sisters of the Japan Province of the Sisters of Notre Dame de Namur. All of these people have helped me to see religious life in a global context and as an international concern.

I wish also to thank Patricia Knopp S.N.D.deN. for her editing assistance and the editors of The Liturgical Press for their help in publishing this text and for their interest in the shape and direction of religious life.

Many others have shaped the questions and commitment which have led to this book. The adequacy of my response to our common concerns can only be measured by whether these reflections speak to the experiences which they have shared and inspire commitment and creativity in their lives and communities. I hope these reflections contribute to a dialogue that helps us all to continue to gain insight into how to choose to be committed.

PART ONE

The Choice Today

CHAPTER ONE

Life Decision in Society

The myth of autonomy

Life needs continuity if it is to succeed. By today's standards, this is a false statement. Continuity suggests obligations and limits. Success in modern society is associated with overcoming limitations and growing free of obligations which hamper personal fulfillment. We live in a society where the promise of unlimited possibilities fuels the American dream.[1]

From an opposite point of view, the open-endedness of modern life is frightening. Ideas such as commitment and continuity can be associated with a lack of interest in a life choice which requires risk. A search for stability can cloak a hidden desire to escape from adult life or never to take up its responsibilities.[2] The longing for stability in this sense is unhealthy.

When escape is their primary motivation, people withdraw before the complexity of modern life by seeking some life style which will protect them from its ambiguities. They give up the task of searching for meaning. Instead, they seek only to carve out their own individual, comfortable life where they do not need to ad-

---

1. For a contemporary discussion of the effects of the American dream on ways of perceiving in its citizens, see: Robert Bellah, *Habits of the Heart: Individualism and Commitment in American Life* (Berkeley: University of California Press, 1985).
2. Erich Fromm, *Escape from Freedom* (New York: Avon Books, 1969).

dress the larger questions of human society and personal meaning. This narrow mentality can be associated with commitment and continuity in life.[3] More often, it proves to be an indication that an individual has given up on life in some significant way. On the surface, this stance appears "normal," but it can be rooted in a deep pessimism regarding what life can offer.

How, then, is it possible to speak of commitment without automatically rejecting it as an act of misguided personal destruction? How can we speak of life in terms of limits without experiencing sour grapes as pessimism regarding the possibilities that life can offer? Certainly, the life choice of religious life is not possible nor well grounded if it reflects either attitude.

The faith community and its tradition offer some clues to help solve this dilemma in its belief about life and the human person. As a community, it has very different views from current society about what is important in life and what it means to be a self-directing person. It questions the typical "self identity" given by today's society. Its own view provides a deeper vision of human life, one necessary both to the understanding of religious life and to sustaining a vowed commitment in our present situation.

We can appreciate the pressures on individuals today as they make vocational choices if we examine how the two contrasting views of human fulfillment, that of the Church and that of society, actually compete for the allegiance of the modern person. Even though there is more encouragement today for adult Christians to form a personal belief system, they must grapple with many conflicts and contradictions in our society to do so. Despite the fact that adult Christians are more independent in their thinking than in previous times, the society retains a powerful influence on them as they come to know who they are and make vocational choices.

It appears, moreover, that many current societal values and attitudes do not support the choice of religious life. This makes religious life incomprehensible based on societal values alone. It can only be understood if the vision of the faith community is blended

---

3. Robert MacAfee Brown addresses this as an aspect of the "Great Fallacy" in *Spirituality and Liberation* (Philadelphia: The Westminster Press, 1988). This problem is related to issues in the woman's movement in Maria Riley, *Transforming Feminism* (Kansas City: Sheed and Ward, 1989).

with the genuine humanitarian aspirations which often draw men and women to it. A faith vision can help individuals break through the myths in our society which offer a false sense of human values. It can challenge the superficial treatment of life's meaning based on the societal values of money and power, self interest, and personal pleasure. This more profound faith vision also provides a deeper understanding of the God-human relationship which is integral to religious life and which supports its meaning and purpose beyond that of the work religious do.

Only this vision of faith, ultimately, grounds the radical way of acting which a vocational decision implies. However, the vision which comes from faith always operates in tension with societal values and the way of life they uphold. Persons who choose religious life thereby enter a contest between two different value systems as they continue to choose their path and deepen in their way of life. We can gain insight into some of the tensions involved in this contest by contrasting the vision of the faith community and that of society regarding a key area of modern life: the meaning of adulthood or the definition of autonomy. The differences between the view of the faith community and that of society have significant bearing on the options which stand before religious today.

Two views of human autonomy

People desire autonomy as an essential element of happiness. Autonomy refers to the possibility and task to determine oneself, that is, to decide what type of person one is going to be, and to be in harmony with the values and norms which one has given oneself.[4] Everyone wants autonomy, but there are many conflicting ideas about what it means.

Both the gospel and the society affirm personal autonomy; however, they do so differently. Scripture portrays personal autonomy as a quality of life which comes from relationship. Society, on the other hand, finds the roots of autonomy in performance. Robert Bellah in *Habits of the Heart* gives one of the best contemporary

4. Franz Bockle, *Fundamental Moral Theology*, trans. by N. D. Smith (New York: Pueblo Publishing Company, 1977) 31.

descriptions of the societal view today.[5] He claims that autonomy in American society is radically tied to the pursuit of individual fulfillment as self-interest. Greater autonomy is associated with upward mobility gained through personal achievement. One advantage of upward mobility in the American mind, is that it brings with it a personal life space, where the man or woman needs to depend less and less on others.

The quest for self fulfillment in itself does not stand in conflict with the gospel vision. However, the difference between the gospel and societal visions lies in what each one means by autonomy and self fulfillment. "I have come that you may have life and have it to the full" can be said by a modern advertising firm as well as by Jesus in the gospel. However, they mean something very different, one from the other. In this chapter, I would like to explore some of the major beliefs of our societal vision of life. In the next chapter, we will compare the societal vision with the vision of the faith community, to show that religious life is rooted in the latter view.

American individualism

One key tension between the gospel and social attitudes is the individualism in American society. To some degree, this individualism can also be found in other first-world societies. In the world view of American society, the individual is the paradigm through which all reality is viewed. In other words, the individual alone is perceived as real. Group and political life, nature and its resources, and even interpersonal relationships and religion are seen dimly as realities in their own right. Their worth is more contingent on their relationship to the fulfillment of the needs and wants of the individual.[6]

This individualism, or the belief that the individual is the only real thing in life, affects the self perception and daily life of the typical

5. Robert Bellah, *Habits of the Heart, op. cit.*
6. For a critique of this attitude, see: Anne E. Carr, *Transforming Grace: Christian Tradition and Women's Experience* (San Francisco: Harper & Row, 1988) especially pp. 128ff., and Johannes Metz, *The Emergent Church*, trans. by Peter Mann (New York: Crossroad, 1986) 82ff.

American. The manner in which communication is approached provides a good example of the influence of individualism on our ways of thinking. There is currently an emphasis on communication in society, not only on sharing wants and desires in "open communication" but also on telling "one's story" in self help groups. Men and women seek healing from others through this style of open communication.

People find, however, that the simple telling of one's personal story is not enough. The weakness in this style of communication is that meaning can only be derived when one can relate one's story to a larger more inclusive one.[7] An individualistic mentality, however, values the individual story primarily. The group story has little meaning. The result is that many people lack a sense of how interpretation of their personal story finds its meaning in a broader story. Radical individualism makes it difficult to incorporate the broader meaning systems of a group or a tradition into a sense of self identity since the self is seen as separate from the group.

An individualistic attitude is also reflected in the tendency to think of the ultimate goals of a good life as matters of personal choice alone.[8] When we hold such an attitude, we measure the success of our lives only by whether the priorities we have chosen have been achieved. In individualistic thinking, our values or priorities cannot be justified by any wider framework of purpose or belief.

When the individual becomes the center of reality in such a radical manner, relationship with the truths of nature, of interpersonal reality, of common tradition and religious meaning have no integral connection to human living. Bellah puts it this way: "American cultural traditions define personality, achievement, and the purpose of human life in ways that leave the individual suspended in glorious, but terrifying isolation."[9] However, if Bellah is right, it is this societal image which provides the most common view of life not only for the public but also for those living and seeking religious life as a vocational choice today.

7. See the section on narrative in Johannes Metz, *Faith in History and Society*, trans. by David Smith (New York: Crossroad, 1980) 205ff.
8. Robert Bellah, *Habits of the Heart*, 22.
9. *Ibid.*, 8.

Relationships beyond the individual

An individualistic climate affects how human relationships, values, harmony with nature and religion are unconsciously viewed at the present time. All are seen as objects of personal choice before they are seen as having value in themselves.[10] This means that we think of self development as occurring in isolation from these relationships rather than through them. There is no harmony with nature that must be achieved for integral human development. Nature is something outside the individual, something to be used for personal fulfillment. There is no overarching value system which reflects what is integral to human fulfillment. There are only idiosyncratic preferences which are adapted based on a cost-benefit calculus.[11]

There are no relationships, such as kinship, friendship, community, and political life, where one *finds* oneself in relationship rather than *chooses* to be in relationship. Relationships are not viewed in the traditional sense in an individualistic framework. They cannot be taken for granted. They are not seen as the stable reference by which one comes to a sense of personal identity.[12]

Religion in American society is also understood in an individualistic climate. Religion is reduced to the expression of the inner feelings of an individual before God. Bellah claims that many Americans believe that institutional Christianity has come to an end. It is going to be replaced by an age of the Spirit in which every individual will be guided by the inner leading of grace without the need of external authority or a faith community.[13] Since religious relationships, like all relationships, are matters of personal choice, they are not stable but are optional. Religious affiliation can be adopted and dropped to the degree it fulfills personal wants and goals.[14]

10. For an explanation of the human experience of value, or the sense "this is important," see: Timothy O'Connell, *Principles for a Catholic Morality*, revised edition (San Francisco: Harper & Row, 1990) chapter 15.

11. For an example of an effort to transcend this type of thinking by integrating a cost-benefit calculus with a broader spectrum of Christian beliefs about life, see: Richard Sparks, *To Treat or Not To Treat?* (New York: Paulist Press, 1988).

12. Robert Bellah, *Habits of the Heart*, chapter 5.

13. *Ibid.*, chapter 9.

14. *Ibid.*, 117–121.

Social life and the individual

Since for Americans, the individual is viewed as the primary reality, society and group life in the United States takes second place to the individual. The individual exists prior to society and separate from it. Americans view society as coming into existence only through the voluntary contract of individuals trying to maximize their own self-interest.

This view of society affects the way we understand freedom. Being free means being free from the influence of others.[15] Freedom is being unconnected. Personal fulfillment is not having other people's values, ideas, or styles of life interfering with one's own. One must be free of the group in order to be able to achieve personal goals. An individualistic mentality tells us we must be free of any group's authority and interference, whether in work, religion, family, or political life.

An individualistic mentality denies all self-definition from group association. To be free is not simply to be left alone by others. It is also to be your own person, in the sense that you have defined who you are, decided for yourself what you want out of life, and are as free as possible from the demands of conformity to family, friends, church, or community. However, since the self is dissociated from the group, once this "freedom from" has been achieved, there is little way in American society to speak of the purpose for which we achieve this quality of life.

What goals should an individual have once he or she has been liberated? Here the culture is silent except to uphold the right of each individual to do whatever he or she chooses to do, as long as he or she does not hurt anyone. This focus on personal freedom, to the exclusion of a vision of what this freedom is for, creates an atmosphere of malaise, or lack of meaning and purpose in the lives of many people.[16] Because the individual is divorced from any wider view of life except that of self-definition, there is an alienation from the broader resources of wisdom which could reflect models of meaning. This individualistic solution leaves a certain emptiness in the American heart.

15. *Ibid.*, 143.
16. Johannes Metz, *The Emergent Church*, 1–15, 67–81.

Achievement of the type of autonomy which society upholds is not without costs. One must be free of bonds to achieve it. For many Americans, freedom means an ability to determine one's life through personal choice in a manner which is unencumbered by others. Upward mobility provides an even greater freedom from restriction. This attitude toward freedom is represented by the American cowboy image: the loner who achieves manhood through his individual efforts against the hostile forces of the Wild West without the support of community and without being related to them in his development.

Effect on work and life-style images

Bellah asserts that even the meaning of work or profession is interpreted in the American mind from an individualistic perspective. For the middle-class person, a career is a course of professional life or employment that offers advancement or honor.[17] A professional career is no longer oriented to any face-to-face community. Rather it is defined by interpersonal standards of excellence, set by a national occupational system. Career development moves one up and away in a life style measured by the success of upward mobility. Profession is no longer conceived of as a calling. A calling involves a man or woman in a function in a community. The more traditional concept of "calling" understands profession in a more relational way. To be a professional involves more than meeting internal standards of performance. It requires incorporation into the civic and civil order of a community.

Community or common life has very little place in the societal view. One reason for this is that therapy is the model of all relationships in an individualistic framework. The one-to-one contact of a counseling relationship of therapy becomes the paradigm for all relationships in American society: intimacy, work, civic, and church involvement. This hidden assumption has serious results in American thinking about group life and its commitments.

Relationships are seen mainly as self-constructed and created for mutual benefit between two people or a group of interest-related others. If the relationship becomes limiting, or the interest which

17. Robert Bellah, *Habits of the Heart*, 119.

formed the group wanes, it can be dropped. The Therapeutic Self is defined by its own wants and satisfaction. Needs and wants are measured by calculating their costs and benefits. This way of thinking leaves a serious vacuum when there is a conflict between individual wants and community needs.

Life-style enclaves

Americans think about community and group life also in an individualistic framework. Group life is not seen in terms of community but rather in terms of pseudo-communities or life-style enclaves. A life-style enclave is different from a community. It is formed by people who share some feature of private life together, rather than sharing many dimensions of daily life. Members of life-style enclaves focus only on those elements of life which they *decide* to share. Enclaves in American society are generally formed around leisure and consumption.

The group is a place where one pursues a private life style, not a shared life.[18] Group living borrows from therapy for its interpersonal rules but draws on no deeper meaning-system or sense of commitment. Virtues for shared living are largely limited to empathic communication, truth-telling and equitable negotiation. This model of relationship has little to say about the nature and purpose of personal, community, or public life, or about the type of commitment needed to sustain it. It is based on the values of enlightened self-interest, a recognized need to collaborate in order to have needs met, and a minimal obligation not to injure.

The effect of this individualistic approach to group life shows up in the group paralysis it creates. Compared to the practices that members of a traditional family, church, town, or religious community share over a lifetime, the therapeutic relationship leaves its members with relatively little to do together except communicate. Patterns of practice—such as ritual, aesthetic, and ethical ways of living together—which define the community as a way of life, are absent.[19] Patterns of commitment which define expectations of loyalty and obligation, which normally keep a community alive, are

18. *Ibid.*, 73.
19. *Ibid.*, 154.

omitted because they require members to examine personal needs in light of the group.

Community and profession versus career and life-style enclave

Religious life exists in an individualistic climate today. However, its belief system is not individualistic. For instance, community and calling are the basis for the communal ideal of the vowed life. The values they uphold are quite different from those of career and life-style enclave. We can see the difference between these ways of thinking if we investigate how each approaches the meaning of work, the resolution of conflict, and the possibility of corporate life. Each area highlights a significant way societal life and religious life are in tension today.

A community and a life-style enclave approach work differently. In a community, face-to-face living is linked to work or to the public nature of the lives of the inhabitants. A community bases its life together on a wider-meaning system. It is concerned with more than leisure and consumption.

Corporate living requires an attitude toward professional life which goes deeper than the individualistic standard of career alone. The value of work is measured by more than a sense of personal accomplishment, rather by its contribution to a community. When the work and the face-to-face living of members of a group have no relationship, there can be no real community life. Without a broader structure of meaning, a group is only the pseudo-community of a life-style enclave.

A community and a life-style enclave have different rules for resolving or not resolving differences among members. In a life-style enclave, differences are avoided or ignored. Since the group is only related in a surface way, members simply walk away from any constructive efforts to work through the conflicts necessary for true relationships. Life remains at the level of surface relationships.

This avoidance of differences is part of the survival technique of the enclave. In a group of potentially conflicting self-interests, with no broader-meaning system, no one can really say that one value system is better than another. Solving conflicts becomes only a matter of technical problem solving, not moral decision making.

In a life-style enclave there is no way to establish rules of a shared life since any rules must remain detached from any social or cultural base that could give them broader meaning. Injunction against certain modes of behavior can only be reduced to matters of personal preference of members of the enclave. It is no surprise then that people avoid differences and relate only in a surface way. People in a life-style enclave are not interdependent, do not act together politically, and do not share a history. Their collective life has only the appearance of community.[20] It is a type of support which serves to differentiate them sharply from those with other life styles and protects them in some way from dissimilar others and the loneliness which comes from our radically individualized society.

We have shown in this chapter, in what I hope is not too much detail, how an individualistic attitude affects the way Americans think about life. It is this social context in which religious life stands today in America and in some other first-world countries. While religious in other parts of the world may not feel these particular cultural tensions, the values of individualism often are the silent partner to material growth. In this, individualism becomes part of the culture of a world market which continues to influence the Church and society, not only materially but culturally as well.

For religious and those aspiring to religious life, individualism colors in an unconscious way how they think about themselves, their life, and their vocational choice. It forms one lens through which religious, as members of their society, view life. The faith community holds that individualism, as a world view, is a myth. It is an inadequate outlook on life. Religious and their communities today need to discern how individualism is inhospitable to some of the deeper realities upon which their life stands. It is this task that we will turn to in the next chapter.

20. *Ibid.*, 71–75.

CHAPTER TWO

Breaking through the Myth

The vowed life involves an entirely different self-definition and perception of life's meaning from that of society. If the societal view of autonomy is right, religious life makes no sense. It requires laying aside the primary pursuit of wealth, power, and arbitrary self-interest which marks the upward mobility of societal autonomy. Instead of moving up and away, the vowed life obliges us to move toward others in relationship and service. It invites us into community to find a personal identity enriched and deepened through the shared identity of the group.

In religious life, a profession is not just a career. It is a calling. While a religious can be highly professional and competent, success is calculated by more than the standards of the occupational system alone. The meaning of professional success is measured by its contribution to the mission of the Church and its service to the life of the people.

The vowed life is communitarian. Community is more than a collection of individuals who live private lives and share only leisure activities and selected interests.[1] Rather, community is a life group where one learns to move out of self toward others in love. Through their vows, religious radically bind their lives not only to God and the people of the Church, but also to the welfare of the concrete others in community. It is a bond which is "another kind of love," sealed not by the genital bonding of marriage but by a bond of affection meant to last a lifetime.

1. Thomas Clarke, S.J., "Jesuit Commitment—Fraternal Covenant?" in *Studies in the Spirituality of the Jesuits*, Vol. III (June, 1971) No. 3, 70–101.

24

A countercultural stance

Religious life involves adopting a countercultural stance both in regard to personal life style and one's idea of success. When religious make a permanent commitment, they challenge the societal attitude that human investments are always provisional. On the contrary, religious life is a response to a primary relationship with God. It is this relationship, which the faith community calls grace, which gives religious life its permanence.

The life of the vows is based on the belief that the meaning of life involves, first and foremost, a response to God in love. This response is not to some external obligation such as the law, but is a response to God in one's deepest self. Understanding life in this way reflects the faith community's approach to human freedom and autonomy, not society's understanding. The vows affirm that we are healthy when we are connected or contingent people, not loners. Our contingency or dependence on God and others is not something to fear. To acknowledge this dependence can bring about a far deeper liberation than individualism can provide.[2]

For the faith community, fulfillment or personal meaning stems from finding a sense of inner truth. A person's inner truth is simply what it means to be the person one was created to be. Religious believe that one way to this truth is reflecting on the life of Jesus Christ.[3] Religious do more than think about Jesus; they enter into the mystery of his own life.

One might say that all Christians believe this, so why take religious vows? It is true that all Christians come to know the truth of life through knowledge of Jesus Christ and the gospel; however, they do so also through a specific vocational structure and set of circumstances. The vows form the perimeter of the life structure of a religious. They provide a way through which a religious integrates all of the dimensions of life in a certain direction through a single life-decision.

2. For an explanation of the role of healthy dependence in Christian conversion, see: Patrick McCormick, *Sin as Addiction* (New York: Paulist Press, 1989). For a criticism of unhealthy dependence, see: Anne Wilson Schaef, *Co-Dependence: Misunderstood-Mistreated* (Minneapolis: Winston, 1986).

3. For a helpful explanation of current thinking on the person of Jesus, see: Elizabeth A. Johnson, *Consider Jesus* (New York: Crossroad, 1990).

The vows are a permanent stance because they serve as the means by which a man or woman will express a personal meaning which takes years to unfold. This sense of meaning may not always be conscious. However, the faith community holds that at a deep level, each person's life has one decisive truth. This truth finds its appropriate expression in a choice meant to last a lifetime.

To understand how such a choice can be made, we will explore in more detail what the faith community believes about human freedom and autonomy.

Another view

The possibility that an ordinary person can make a good vocational decision is based on a view of the world and the human person different from that of society. The faith community believes that there is more to being a person than achieving outward success in society. Upward mobility is not enough to satisfy the deeper human need to transcend self and to love. The call to love and transcendence involves more than the self-initiation of personal plans and goals. It requires a response to a person's deepest identity.

Created by God, each person has at the core of his or her life the reality of God's own presence. It is God's presence, essentially linked to each one's true self, which is the source of the call to transcendence.[4] We can create our lives because we have first been created by God, and God's presence dwells within us. Real creativity in life comes from God's call from within to respond to the mystery of our lives.

It takes faith to recognize that the deepest truth of being a person is the presence of a true self, a self which is deeper than personal accomplishments. It is only by recognizing this truth and the need for faith that people can begin to understand the meaning of their lives. God's presence in our innermost being gives each of us a personal vocation. The desire to live in relationship with God according to the truth of our own personality is the starting point of any vocational awareness.

4. Juan Luis Segundo, *Grace and the Human Condition*, trans. by John Drury (New York: Orbis Books, 1973) 127ff. Karl Rahner develops this theme in *Foundations of Christian Faith* (New York: Seabury, 1978) especially chapters 1–4.

When we recognize that we have a true self within, we begin to have real freedom. Theologians use the term "freedom" to describe the distinct experience of being human. Freedom is the positive relationship to oneself that makes becoming oneself a possible goal of human life. Once we recognize that our identity is deeper and truer than the surface definition of society suggests, something more than a sense of independence grows in our life. A self-possession emerges which allows us to recognize that our unique personality and personal truth actually are a legitimate path to becoming fully human.[5]

For a member of the faith community, to be in touch with God at the center of one's life is at the heart of personal integrity. Any sense of autonomy and vocation is based on this awareness of God-within. While all people can experience this personal center as mystery, for the Christian, this mystery has a name, the God of Jesus Christ. Inherent to the recognition of being called beyond ourselves is the sense that real meaning and growth is dependent on our response to this experience of God.

The faith community's alternate vision of human life is that our lives are more than they appear to be, taken at face value. They are a mystery, because we share in God's mystery. This mystery is one of relationship. God is and chooses to be essentially related to us. This is the meaning of grace. Grace is the unmerited reality of God's free decision to relate to us and the resulting effect it has on the meaning of our lives.

Freedom as a response

In contrast to the view that freedom means being free from the influence of others in order to pursue self interest, the faith com-

5. Juan Luis Segundo, *Grace and the Human Condition*, 30. The experience of the pull of the surface definitions of self from society may come in many forms: an idea of success, peer pressure, family expectations, or internalized personal goals unsuited to one's real gifts or abilities. For a commentary on the struggle for identity in American life, see: Madonna Kolbenschlag, *Lost in the Land of Oz* (San Francisco: Harper & Row, 1988). For another approach, see: Jean-Marc Laporte, *Patience and Power: Grace for the First World* (New York: Paulist Press, 1988) 1–30.

munity sees freedom or autonomy as the self-possession necessary to respond to the full meaning of life.

In this light, autonomy is the capacity for self-determination or the power to develop one's life. Like the society, the faith community believes autonomy grows through making choices, but they value a different kind of choice. Autonomy grows from choosing between being open toward others and loving or withdrawing into self in self-preoccupation. Real autonomy is not upward mobility which brings less and less need to live interdependently with others. Rather, autonomy consists ultimately in the power to give direction to one's life in the face of the inner call to love or to refuse to do so. At its most basic level, autonomy cannot be equated with any accomplishment or action or status achieved in life. Rather, these choices have meaning only if they are a reflection of a deeper stance of our person.

Religious life is based on this view of autonomy. Religious in novels and movies search for a "spiritual" world which lies hidden in a convent, external to the person. Real religious respond to an awareness that this spiritual world lies within them at the deepest level of personal life. Religious commitment involves recognition of God at the heart of life and expresses the desire to respond to that presence in a radical way.

In this sense, to choose to live according to religious vows involves a prior choice of self. It involves a choice of the kind of "self" the person is going to be. Am I going to move outward toward others in love or withdraw into self-preoccupation? This choice of self is prior to the choice of any course of action in life. Rather, it is a choice to construct oneself in freedom within the real possibilities of this moment or to turn away from this process in self-absorption.

Hence, when religious commit themselves to a vowed life, they make a prior statement about themselves and the orientation of their lives. Inner freedom makes this possible.[6] They choose to love or not to love *before* choosing a special manner of loving. Understanding this sense of freedom is important for grasping the meaning of a vocational choice because it points to the most fundamental

---

6. Another name for inner freedom is basic freedom or transcendental freedom. See "Freedom" in *Encyclopedia of Theology: The Concise Sacramentum Mundi*, ed. by Karl Rahner (New York: Seabury, 1975) 533ff.

choice which the vows symbolize. The fundamental choice to use freedom to love is true autonomy for the faith community.

Another way to understand inner freedom or autonomy is to compare it to the talent or sum of money mentioned in the gospel parable. The critical choice in that story was not how to invest the talent. Rather it was the decision to invest at all. The crisis presented in the parable was the crisis of risk.

Would each person invest this sum of money received as a gift, or would they bury it out of fear? The choice of inner freedom presents a similar crisis to that surrounding the talent. Through freedom we decide whether the direction of our lives will be one of investment in the concerns of others and God. Or we can choose a life of disinvestment. We can stand on the fringe of life waiting until we can be sure we will not be hurt by getting involved. We can decide to bury our talent of freedom in self-preoccupation and egotism.

The meaning of inner freedom suggests that the freedom which lies at the heart of a life choice is more than one action, such as the initial decision to make vows. It is more than the sum of all the subsequent decisions which follow in the life of a religious. Rather, it underlies them, permeates them, and goes beyond them, without ever being actually one of them.

Inner freedom is expressed, however, in all these ways. Primarily it can be experienced in a fundamental commitment whereby persons state before God, to themselves, and to the community that the direction of their lives will be lived faithfully according to the vows of a particular community. It is to this promise that religious may often return throughout their lives for a renewed sense of direction and purpose.

Commitment for a lifetime

The faith community's belief that a life choice is possible and can endure is grounded on its belief about freedom. It sees a lifetime as a process whereby a person interprets the meaning of his or her call to freedom and expresses it through concrete decisions. Each person is called to decide a "course" for the freedom to take. This "course" gives unity to life and direction to the many individual choices which come through the years.

In the face of all those things which run contrary to this course, one's own inconsistency, or the pressures and vicissitudes of life itself, the person is meant to affirm his or her own personal truth. The community holds that in the face of obstacles the person must endure or prevail or lose that truth about the self which he or she has come to know.

In this sense, a commitment is not some pressure externally imposed upon us. Rather, fidelity to a commitment is key to becoming a person. The faith community can affirm this possibility because it believes the potential to do it lies within each person.[7] However, the potential for commitment needs community support. The faith community sees that its own role is to support people in their commitment and to continue to share the faith vision and relationships which help sustain it.

The potential to make a commitment is given in the gift of freedom, but the ability to do so grows through the years. Even the personal self-awareness that leads someone to make a commitment builds up over time, before it proves to be a sufficient source upon which to base a life choice.[8] A life decision involves the personal capacity to choose, to prefer one thing to another. This requires not only the free exclusion of certain possibilities and a preference for others, but also the personal stability to risk making a judgment or estimate. Such a process takes maturity and involves choices which can never be confirmed absolutely.[9]

Given all these realities, the faith community still holds that it is possible to make a life commitment. This is a countercultural stance in a society that sees goals and relationships as temporary and fleeting. In contrast, the community claims that men and women, as centers of meaning, have a certain freedom over or "from" themselves and dominion over the world. We are capable of the self-possession required for free choice. This type of freedom is something which does not come automatically, but involves struggle and sacrifice.

7. Klaus Demmer, "The Irrevocable Decision: Thoughts on the Theology of Vocation," *Communio* Vol. 1 (1974) 297.

8. *Ibid.*, 295.

9. Margaret Farley wrestles with this issue of commitment in *Personal Commitments: Beginning, Keeping, Changing* (San Francisco: Harper & Row, 1986).

However, this freedom is also a "freedom to." Through it, we have the possibility to shape our lives in spite of the many limits which make up being human. This freedom shows up as the possibility of shouldering, little by little and with repeated setbacks, a control over a life process whose problems and limits continue to remain in force.

The faith community's belief in the possibility of commitment is not for superhuman people or just for perfect situations. Freedom is not an escape from the limitations and problems of real life and relationships. It is not some ideal capacity which operates independently of the pressures of the real world. No one becomes free once he or she finds a situation in life or society where there are no constraints or limits. Rather, the faith community knows that the reality of many aspects of human life today always limits human freedom in some way. The fact that we are free does not remove these obstacles totally. Instead, obstacles and personal limitations always challenge us and form the stuff from which decisions take life.

This struggle with the limits found in life generally proves true in the course of any vowed commitment. In religious life, it is really only the unexpectedness of real life that deepens a commitment and ultimately gives shape to its outlines. No one can know all of life's contingencies from the outset. Rather, to make vows is simply to begin on a journey which is comprised partially of the unknown. In the next chapter we will explore some further dimensions of this journey.

CHAPTER THREE

A Vocational Sign: The Capacity to Be Countercultural

To make and sustain a vowed commitment presupposes that a basic level of freedom is already operative in a person's life. While all people are free or have within themselves their own sufficient reason to be, not all people use the capacities of their freedom. Even after we begin to develop our freedom with more seriousness, we always are free to a greater or lesser degree.

Jesus understood this. We see this awareness in his own understanding of his mission: "I have come that you may have life and have it to the full." Freedom is part of the fullness of life to which he calls us. Jesus understood also that we have to choose to be free; freedom isn't automatic. The gospels affirm that the fullness of freedom is something that no one has all at once. It comes only through a process of openness and effort. The struggle is portrayed as the search for the pearl of great price, which requires that we sell all for its purchase.

Freedom and its consequences

Only real people in real situations have freedom. Most people do not think of freedom in the abstract; rather, they reflect on the results of free choice in their lives. When freedom operates, there are always results. At times, the positive results are invisible to the eye; however, over the long term, even these small internal victories of freedom begin to show. A change in facial expression, a new attitude in a community, a shift in a legal policy. The Scriptures call these positive types of results, the "fruits" of love. A negative use of freedom also has results. These results are sin. Sin also can be invisible to the eye. But it, too, over the long term, does not remain hidden. Even sin which is committed in our hearts eventually will express itself in action. The Scriptures tell us that deceits, jealousies, selfishness never remain just in our hearts; eventually they cripple our lives together.

Sin can never be detached from its concrete results, since it, like love, is an act of freedom. At times sin blends in so much with our lives that its results only appear hidden. Acts of love which resist its power always bring out sin's presence. This explains why a positive use of freedom often involves "the cross." It is the pain we experience when we try to love as Jesus did in the real world, against our own tendencies to allow its negativity and our own to overtake us.

Sin also gets embedded in our world. While all people have freedom, some people's main experience of life is tainted with the suffering caused by the freedom of others. Our culture holds within it both the positive and negative results of our freedom. The negative results get into the life of our institutions and our ways of thinking. When we seek to love in a manner which is not affirmed generally in our culture or, in the institutions in which we live and work, we feel the weight of it pulling us in an opposite direction. For this reason, to act out of freedom in a positive manner often involves the power to be countercultural.

Taking a countercultural stance

Since freedom produces results, we can also say something about what its positive results in love produce over the long term. The faith community believes that a positive use of freedom creates a world which is more human or more suitable to the dignity of human beings. Freedom, over the long term, is basically transformative. A positive use of freedom however requires the ability to step outside the social frameworks which are convenient, but less than they could be, and dedicate ourselves to the creation of alternatives.

This has important consequences for considering religious life or ongoing commitment. Since a religious vocation is always lived out amid the conflicts of real life, the readiness to respond to and live out a vocational choice requires the capacity to be countercultural. In earlier forms of religious life the capacity to be countercultural was evidenced in the ability to physically "leave the world." By withdrawing into a monastic framework the religious witnessed to a radical Christian life. However, today the call to be countercultural is lived out in direct interaction with the culture. Because of this fact, a religious needs to be more aware of how the internal capacities of freedom are related to a choice of religious life and the type of countercultural stance required by his or her vocation.

We can get insight into the level of freedom needed for a choice of religious life by looking at the capacities which are usually considered to be signs that a person is using his or her freedom in a healthy and whole manner. In doing so, we can also see the direction of growth which can indicate that a person is adopting a countercultural stance. Both lines of thinking will show that to live out a vowed commitment is to develop one's life along lines which are different from what society dictates.

Freedom and commitment

Freedom involves the capacity to view life as a center of meaning. We have the power to understand the world and other people as separate, as something distinct from ourselves. Freedom involves the capacity to separate ourselves from the world and to experience ourselves as subjects, or unique persons before God.[1] This ability is essential to take up responsibility for our lives and the world around us. In order to know a reality as independent from us it is necessary to know where we end and where reality begins.

The faith community believes that such a quality of self-awareness is necessary for a vocational commitment. People who merge so totally with their work, another person, the group, or societal expectations of power, wealth, and status lack this capacity. In order to make and sustain a commitment as a religious, it is necessary to have the ability to stand on one's own.

1. The notion of a subject in relationship to the world is explored in Johannes Metz, *Faith in History and Society*, 60ff. For a less technical presentation, see: Richard Gula, *Reason Informed by Faith: Foundations of Catholic Morality* (New York: Paulist Press, 1989) 68ff.

Freedom also involves the capacity for self-reflection. This is the ability, in a limited manner, to distance oneself sufficiently from oneself that self-reflection can occur. The faith community believes that we have the potential to reflect on our relationships and our acts. It is through this process that the growth in self-awareness occurs which ultimately helps us to make decisions about our lives and the surrounding world.

A habit of self-reflection is needed to make a commitment to the vowed life and to sustain it. Religious need the ability to put aside work or a social schedule which leaves little time for reflection. While on the surface a life with no time for prayer or serious thinking can appear to reflect ''being needed'' or ''being involved'' or ''being popular,'' it can also connote an unwillingness to face the deeper questions of life in general and one's own life in particular. Drifting by the larger questions of life or refusing to name the loneliness and anxiety which feed over-activity are both ''escapes from freedom.''[2] They are mechanisms by which we give up an aspect of our freedom and hence hinder its other capacities.

A habit of self-reflection alone, however, is inadequate to effect change in our lives or in the world. Many people are involved in all types of self-awareness projects, yet their lives never seem to take any direction or have any purpose. Even though self-knowledge is essential so that we can attribute meaning to life experience, it is not enough.

In addition to the capability for separateness, the ability to attribute meaning, and the capacity to reflect, we have to act and give our lives some type of concrete form and direction. To do this, we exclude some options in order to prefer others, and live with the consequences. This requires personal discipline that shows itself not in aimless self-denial but in the capacity ''to give up'' in order to ''be for.''[3]

The ability to face exclusion and preference is not just a skill needed to *enter* religious life. It has to be called upon throughout the years of commitment. It is one way that religious give real attention to their vocation throughout a lifetime.[4] We assess and

2. Erich Fromm, *Escape from Freedom, op. cit.*
3. M. Scott Peck enlarges on this theme in *The Road Less Traveled* (New York: Simon and Schuster, 1978).
4. Margaret Farley, *Personal Commitments*, especially chapter 4.

measure the alternatives which come into our lives from the perspective of preference for those which reaffirm our life direction. In this way, religious live out their vocation in faith. Some choices are thereby excluded, not because they are bad, but because they do not fit.

After many such experiences, we can arrive at a deeper insight into the freedom at the heart of our commitment. We learn that we can be happy even though all alternatives are not chosen. This can be the case if religious freely make choices around a life project. Alternatives that they themselves consciously choose are then expressions of their own deepest desires.

Meaning in life comes from more than the ability to set goals and achieve them. We must be able to receive meaning from those who have gone before, from the community as a whole, and from the truth of reality. A thief could have the power of exclusion and preference and use it to become adept at stealing. Yet most people would judge that thieves do not have the content in their lives worthy of human pursuit.

For a Christian, this "received" meaning is contained in the life of Jesus Christ. To make vows is to state that Jesus Christ is the Word who reveals the content of what it means to be a fully human person. To make a vowed commitment and grow in it requires the ability to be a hearer of the Word and not only a speaker of it. This ability shows itself in the capacity to be a person in dialogue with the truth of daily life, the word, and the community.

This point is essential for understanding the capacity to make a vowed commitment. The commitment to the vows is secondary, the choice of a path. The choice to be a religious must reflect a prior human choice "to be" at all. This choice "to be" is essentially a choice to transcend self, to move out of the posture of egotism and to open oneself to God, to reality, and to others in love. We essentially choose to be open to God's ongoing revelation in all of these dimensions. The vows reaffirm this choice and give it a social context and a sense of direction and content.[5]

The continued living out of the vows also must reflect this choice "to be" in all its concreteness. As a path alone, religious

---

5. A good explanation of vocation and adult commitment in a social context is in James P. Hannigan, *Homosexuality: The Test Case For Christian Sexual Ethics* (New York: Paulist Press, 1988) chapter 4, "Sexuality and Vocation."

life in itself can offer no validity to a human life. Rather, the vows must reflect our ability to love in openness to others and to reality. It is only this exercise of freedom in love which can be a means of self-fulfillment.

The society holds that to become autonomous we must achieve individuality, separate ourselves from others, and leave home. The capacity to be an individual is seen differently by the faith community. It is a capacity for commitment. In the view of society, autonomy means an even greater expansion of options and a freedom from the influence of others. This implies a definition of individuality which almost precludes enduring commitment. In the faith community, autonomy includes an acceptance of individuality based not only on outward achievement but on inner awareness. Individuality in this sense prefigures commitment.

Individuality and commitment

How can this be? To be an individual is to experience being this person—with this history, with these gifts and faults—and not another. Uniqueness or individuality contains a fundamental limitation. I cannot be anyone else. I can only be myself. The paradox is that the experience of this limitation contains a promise. Embracing the uniqueness of one's one-and-only life and deciding to love despite one's limitations, brings fulfillment.[6]

In a fundamental way, acceptance of individuality is an acceptance of a type of death. It is an experience of the paschal mystery, embracing death for resurrection. This choice requires hope. To choose to be oneself before God is to hope this is enough for happiness.

A vowed commitment is a similar type of choice. It too is a choice made in hope. The profession of vows is a choice of a "path" and acceptance of limits. It is a statement of love which holds that in the process of the limitation of options, I will find the fulfillment of my deepest desires. One sign of readiness for a vowed commitment is the capacity for uniqueness, for it implies a willingness to accept limitation. To view life in this way is truly countercul-

6. Klaus Demmer, "The Irrevocable Decision: Thoughts on the Theology of Vocation," *op. cit.*, 297.

tural for it affirms a type of birth from death that society cannot address.[7]

As a religious continues in his or her commitment this sense of uniqueness is not erased. Rather, it is intensified. Through decisions which require preference for some things and exclusion of others, a religious confronts necessary restrictions, a type of death. A person does so, however, as a free choice. The ongoing experience of choosing one path over another deepens the person in his or her choice. The need for hope continues, and the experience that death is for resurrection becomes true in ever-new ways.

In our lives as religious, there can be many crises when the sense of restriction seems more apparent than the positive and necessary role of limits. The ability to come to terms with one's deepest desires can provide a sense of direction through the crisis. Someone who has accepted his or her uniqueness at a deep level already has experienced that becoming *someone* requires that one cannot become *everyone*.

When this capacity is not present, it is difficult to separate what is central from what is peripheral to a vocational experience and to reconnect with the self one affirmed and set on its course in the making of vows. (A religious can easily get lost depending upon the degree to which what must be "set aright" is outward or inward to self.)[8]

Ongoing fidelity is also difficult if we only rely on our personal strength alone. A vocation is a dialogue. This means that a vocation is constantly given. Religious need to experience God as faithful in a manner which makes up for their limits. The experience of God, giving to us and dialoging with us, helps us to respond to a call which is given, not only earned. Without the experience that God continues to call, support, and reveal, religious can gradually experience less and less moral challenge in their vocation.

A sense of self built only on personal power and talents can feed a crippling egotism. In a crisis, we can be blind to issues of responsibility to others—important to the nature of the vows and the meaning of life affirmed by them—if personal needs alone are the focus of discernment.[9] Ongoing awareness of the presence of

7. M. Scott Peck, *The Road Less Traveled*, 72.
8. Margaret Farley, *Personal Commitments*, 90ff.
9. Klaus Demmer, *op. cit.*, 300.

God can help to focus concerns in a more relational and connected framework which ultimately can help religious integrate long-term commitments and personal needs.

A final sign that the freedom necessary for a commitment to religious life is present is the ability to build a community which has an outward focus. The faith community believes that people grow through service to a community which also reaches out to others. Autonomy as self-interest is not enough. Rather, respect for the dignity of others and concern for the welfare of society as a whole are more important than a life centered on personal interests alone.

The society sees this type of involvement as the death of freedom, because involvement with others necessitates a limit to options. The faith community believes that true freedom is freedom in relationship. Freedom without limitations does not exist, nor does freedom from the influence of others. Real freedom is a call to investment.

For the faith community, a healthy society is more than the stage on which individuals experience the drama of life. Group life is not the result of placing together already "finished" individuals. Rather than being external to us, these relationships form part of our lives and self-understanding. To contribute to community and society is an essential part of human fulfillment. Because of this fact, attention to the quality of life in our environment and in the world is important to the faith community's view of a meaningful and committed life.

Capacity for realistic bonding

We are not the lone cowboys of society's image of the individual. Rather we grow and come to be through the society. In many ways, we are dependent on it. However, society is not something which comes ready made in our lives. It is something which must be shaped by our freedom. This raises the issue of what realistic bonding means. If the capacity to contribute to a larger whole is a sign of readiness for a life commitment, then the specifics of this ability need to be made clear.

When the faith community holds up the values of bonding with others and contributing to society, it does not suggest an uncritical approval of the group over the individual. Rather, all social arrangements from a family to a social system are specific ways of approaching human relationships. All have to be approached critically. To bond with others does not mean being a doormat.

All institutions are open to change since they reflect specific ways of conceiving of human relationships which have alternatives. Realistic bonding involves the readiness to build relationships. It also involves the capacity to change human relationships which are dehumanizing through the changing of institutions which structure and perpetuate these relationships. To be able to bond with others in community and society does not mean a passive adjustment to the status quo.

Realistic bonding also means that we contribute to the dreams and vision of a group, yet also critically reflect on its prevailing ways of thinking. All groups have a system of beliefs, laws, and values which legitimate the existing ways people relate to one another. It is naive to think that the prevailing ideas in any group favor change in the group life or will naturally benefit those who are marginated.

Realistic bonding involves an ability to support and identify with a community, yet to critique it. It is necessary that we identify how the way we think helps or hinders our group purpose or the growth of community members. Since all groups and societies have an informal system of beliefs, identifying and examining beliefs is an ongoing dimension of any type of community life. While the society and the group always place a certain limit on our freedom, we transform our lives by transforming this very group and society. The capacity to do this over the long term is a vital sign of a religious vocation.

Summary: the heart of a vocational decision

The story—or the history—of the decisions we make over a lifetime has a greater meaning than the simple retelling of the succession of isolated acts which are not linked together. Rather, each personal history contains an inner meaning. At the core of the life of each of us is a center of self which endures and continues throughout all the changes and transitions in life.

A vocational decision has at its root the intention to express our personal truth in a practical choice.[10] We live the vows in the interdependence of community, in which we continue to discover and express our personal meaning. The limits implied in this interdependence are the base from which true personal meaning and maturity is achieved. It is the capacity to live these basic beliefs of the faith community that determines our readiness for a vocational commitment and constantly feeds its development.

10. For a fuller explanation, see: Josef Fuchs, "Basic Freedom and Morality" in *Introduction to Christian Ethics*, ed. by Ronald P. Hamel and Kenneth R. Himes, O.F.M. (New York: Paulist Press, 1989).

PART TWO

Issues of Transition

CHAPTER FOUR

From Identity to Transformation

The journey

If we look over the last twenty years in religious life, there is one value that has been affirmed in an unmistakable way—the value of the person. This affirmation has not just been verbal but has been institutionalized at every level of religious life. The focus on the value of the person—perhaps more than any other value—symbolizes from an internal perspective the changed context in religious life that we have experienced since the council.

However, the notion of the person that has been affirmed has not come from a single source. Consciously and unconsciously, this same emphasis has been imbibed both in the Church and in the culture. The renewal in directed retreats and charismatic prayer has provided a spiritual vision of this same reality.

The theology of the Vatican Council and the new perspectives in Scripture and liturgy in the Church have also fed this movement. Religious have learned from the arts. They have found Jesus in literature and in the Christ of Fellini. Liturgical music has taken on the rhythms and instruments of the day and voiced the concerns of persons.

Congregations have adapted the person-centered management ideas from business and extensively utilized both classical and popular psychology in assisting members to come to a better self-understanding. They have changed their financial policies and developed a more personalized budgeting system.

Communication techniques have been developed and wholistic health consciousness has been promoted. The specialization and professionalization of work, which in part is reflective of the emphasis on the person in our society, have also become part of the lives of religious as well.

The emphasis on the person has also been critical. We have turned to the critiques of the social system highlighted in the late sixties and carried on by many church groups and civic movements in the seventies and eighties. Civil rights, multicultural integration, environmental stewardship, peace, the Third World, and poverty have also been our concerns because they address the possibilities of others to be persons. These movements have forced us to examine our attitudes and beliefs.

Some people have found that the Women's Movement has refined their notion of the type of person they want to become and the type of society they want to build. Many people have found help from these movements in clarifying their self and communal definition and their image of the better world to which the gospel calls them.

However, the many sources from which religious have drawn to support their affirmation of the person have not always agreed on what a person is. At times, their images of person have seemed contradictory. Religious have allowed their culture to teach them as they have been encouraged by Vatican II. Good gardeners, these movements have pruned and fertilized congregations. They have grown.

We have been shade to each other and have been fruitful. We know what it means to be a water-bearing cactus in the deserts of ministry and life. Some have imaged sturdy pines withstanding the emotional and health storms of injustice and the life cycle. Others have been uprooted by the violent winds of life, leaving some broken, needing props and gentle care to survive. Saplings have grown among us and favorite oaks have fallen. Religious men and women know these years, and these movements have touched them.

However, as these years and movements have whacked off excesses and fed undernourished areas of our lives, many religious have not been sure if they have offered an integrated vision of the person they have sought to promote. Hence, at this time religious again struggle to create a center of value in themselves and in their congregations from which they can direct further growth.

Symptoms of the search for a center

The search for a center of value is also a search for common meaning in religious congregations. While the last twenty-five years have been filled with exploration, they have not provided time for sifting through stories to find the common meaning that they hold for the future.

Since the Vatican Council, religious orders have organized to be open to the plurality of meaning-systems the period of renewal has created. They have strained to protect individual freedom and to create a climate of tolerance. However, they have been less successful in creating a common vision and some criteria by which the validity of their lives can be measured.

Common vision is needed for future direction. The lack of criteria makes it difficult to determine which experiences are inconsistent with a congregation's identity or incompatible with its mission. The result is that, for some, religious identity has become so elastic that it has lost its meaning.

Mary Jo Leddy refers to this phenomenon as the development of the liberal model of religious life.[1] It reflects the high priority placed on the individual in congregations since the Vatican Council. A liberal model or outlook is based on the assumption that the development of the individual will result automatically in a common good. This stands in contrast to a conservative approach where group identity is fostered mainly through centralized laws.

An integrated vision of the whole is not extremely important to the liberal model. Stress on common purpose is seen as a limitation to freedom. In the place of a commonly held social vision to which all hold themselves accountable, members make decisions by the facilitation of opposing interests in conflict resolution. Greater pluralism is created by this model, but at the cost of a loss of a sense of common direction.

The search of religious congregations for a more relevant life and ministry is reflected in the liberal model. Like individuals in search of meaning in the throes of change, they have struggled to arrive at a new sense of identity. They have left behind set ways of doing things and have reached out to new values.

---

1. Mary Jo Leddy, "Beyond the Liberal Model," *The Way*, Supplement 65 (Summer, 1989) 40–53.

A parallel to this process can be seen in the life of any individual in the normal maturation process. It is a search which involves trial and error. However, to be successful, the process also requires that a person test his or her experience. Various satisfactions in life have to be weighed and compared. Ultimately, some have to be chosen and others rejected.[2]

The liberal model allows for this first step—the trial and error search—in acquiring new values, but it is less successful dealing with the second step, the testing of experience. The reason for this lack is that the liberal model follows a liberal view of the world. This outlook assumes that unlimited choices are possible. Hence there is little reason to close off options.[3]

It is easy to see why the liberal mentality was attractive to religious congregations as they went through renewal. They were eager to reach out to the possibilities that such an open atmosphere held out to them. They saw the possibilities before them and took the risks necessary to achieve a renewed sense of identity. These risks have been essential for the construction of a new meaning-system in light of Vatican II.

The crisis that religious congregations face today is that of sorting out and prioritizing their values. Eventually, some values have to be subordinated to others in the face of a unifying goal. In the congregation's life, just as in the life of every person, it is inevitable that prioritizing has to be done.

Choices can be made even though there is no way to assure that goals chosen are really worth the cost of relinquishing others. A type of focus can be drawn even though there is never enough time in life to test all possibilities. The liberal outlook seems to hide these life realities from congregations. This postpones growth. Yet the faith upon which religious life is based demands this limiting process.

2. Juan Luis Segundo reflects on the faith required for this process in *Faith and Ideologies*, trans. by John Drury (New York: Orbis Books, 1982) chapter 1. See also Roger Haight, S.J., *Dynamics of Theology* (New York: Paulist Press, 1990) chapter 1.

3. For an explanation of a liberal model or approach, see: Joe Holland and Peter Henriot, S.J., *Social Analysis: Linking Faith and Justice* (Washington: Center of Concern, 1980) 14–15.

The inherent call of faith

It is not just the external realities of decline in numbers or limited financial resources which demand this limiting process, but the nature of the faith upon which religious life is built. Faith is the basis on which every person reaches out in love to mystery beyond themselves. Faith enables us to entrust our lives to discipleship of Jesus through the charism of our particular religious congregation.

The crisis facing religious and their congregations today is connected to the faith which is the source of their life. The solution is not simply to have faith. It is more a question of *how to structure* expressions of faith to transform the Church and the world in order to pass on this faith to the next generation. All faith has a practical meaning. Belief contains a call to lifegiving action. One particular type of action called forth from congregations today is that of generativity, action which concerns the next generation and the common good.

The call to prioritize

Congregations face a challenge similar to that faced by any adults who make choices to be generative. A young couple wishing to have a child has to be ready to forgo certain aspects of their social life in order to begin their family. The steps for a congregation to become generative are similar to those in a human growth pattern.

On a personal level, we develop a sense of personal values and set goals. Next, we learn to structure our life around our values. We have to learn what other values help develop our chosen values and to what extent they do so. For example, a young professional may have to get a new job in order to better support another child. Such parents learn through experience what price they are willing to pay for a partial achievement of goals and what price is so high that it means the destruction of the very goals they are seeking.[4] Congregations today are faced with the same task.

For individuals to be generative, the assumption that unlimited options are possible has to be left behind, along with the other loved but no-longer-useful souvenirs of adolescence. The same type of process and honesty is needed in congregations today. Continu-

4. Juan Luis Segundo, *Faith and Ideologies*, 8.

ing with the liberal model of renewal has a cost. Its price is a loss of meaning which is brought about by using it, not as a transitional and healing tool, but as an end in itself. Religious are asking today if it is a price which is too high for the freedoms it promises.

The call for practical wisdom

Generative action also requires the ability to face reality and let go of illusions. For religious congregations, this means the capacity to acknowledge the real condition of religious life today and to enter into a creative search regarding how to make their communal faith effective in the current situation. Religious need a new type of practical wisdom in order to do this. As communities, we need to know the best and most economical way to combine the meaning of our essential foundations with the know-how to manipulate the boundaries of our reality.

Practical wisdom is the capacity to be double visioned. It is the ability to have one eye on the alternatives and another on the real limits which focus congregational responsibilities. Communities are acting with practical wisdom when they can put the two together and "see," in a concrete decision, where "what can be" and "what is" can be brought together.

We need the ability to grasp the present moment and reflect on it critically. This requires the willingness to dig deep to examine whether the ground of our congregational assumptions is still fertile. Can the future be planted in our ground? Is it suitable for the environmental pressures of the next millennium? Or is it worn out by the chemicals of world views that were suitable for the flourishing of past seasons of religious life? In the future could these attitudes destroy its soil?

The call to center congregational energies at this point of renewal is not simply a need demanded by diminishing numbers and dwindling financial resources. Such an assumption supposes that a miracle in development efforts or vocation recruitment could allow congregations to continue as usual without any inherent alteration in their mode of proceeding. On the contrary, these external difficulties are great graces. They reflect the limiting, focusing investment in love which is integral to the meaning of religious life. They force the generative choices essential for congregations to build the future.

The crisis of generativity

The capacity to transform or to invest in some common social vision makes a person or group able to move creatively into the future. On a personal level, this is the capacity for generativity, the ability to emotionally invest in the future, especially in the next generation. Generativity is more than being productive. It involves the ability to care for and nurture what has already been created.[5]

Its opposite, stagnation, is the inability to maintain an interest in the offshoots of one's generativity, whether it be children or work. Instead, self-absorption and preoccupation with individual needs replace the outward movement toward the needs of others. The result is a loss of interest, respect, or compassion for those for whom we are responsible.

Generativity can be distinguished from other types of involvement and busyness. An adult can be interested in life, be involved in many activities, but not have interest in the next generation or in the deeper elements of life which require long-term commitment and investment.

What marks true generativity is the willingness to participate in a broader social vision, whether this be of family, community, or nation. To this vision, one subordinates personal interests. Such an investment links a person to a social or cosmic network of care. It is this network which sustains a person in making a continual emotional investment beyond personal interests, despite setbacks and disappointments. In this process, the pull of apathy in life is counteracted by the spiritual breakthrough brought about through generativity. Without this breakthrough, apathy grows and is fed by the inability to be concerned about the distress of others.[6]

Magicians or priests

Groups can be identified by their ability to be generative. One way to measure the effects of the religious beliefs of a group is by its ability to stimulate this generative outlook. Max Weber, a sociologist, has stated that a main indicator of how religion actually functions in a community is its capacity to lead that community

5. Donald Capps, *Deadly Sins and Saving Virtues* (Philadelphia: Fortress Press, 1987) 58–70.
6. *Ibid.*, 106–109.

to transform itself. Weber likened the role of religion to that of a magician or a priest. He did not compare priests and magicians as individuals, but used them as symbols of the way religion can influence the life of a group.

A magician does not lead a community to transform itself or to reach out to the new challenges called forth by changes in the environment. Rather, the magician manipulates the gods to conform to the expectations of the people as they are now. When religion functions as a magician, it comforts but offers no challenge.

A priest, on the other hand, leads a community to transformation—to face and then adapt to the perplexities of a new environment. The priest calls the community to change. He or she challenges the community to leave behind its self-centered desires to resist the calls of reality in its life. The priest uses the sacred rituals of religion to remind the group of their need to move outward, and links them with the transcendent vision necessary to do so.[7] When religion functions as a priest, it challenges as well as comforts.

Generativity and the liberal model of religious life

The liberal or therapeutic model of religious life is criticized today for its inability to generate a common vision.[8] Without a common vision, generative action is difficult. Using Weber's analysis, we could question at what point religious life takes on a magical quality rather than a priestly direction.

The pre-Vatican institutional model of religious life did generate a common vision. It did so with the help of systems of common life. The liberal model, however, was developed primarily for the nurturance of the personal dimensions in religious life which were not addressed in pre-Vatican structures. The main thrust of this approach is to create an atmosphere of tolerance and pluralism in order to allow individual members the fullest amount of freedom to develop, a freedom which the previous model did not allow.[9]

7. For a commentary on Weber's thought on this point, see: Gregory Baum, *Religion and Alienation* (New York: Paulist Press, 1975) 86ff.
8. Mary Jo Leddy, *op. cit.*, 44.
9. *Ibid.*, 46.

Since it is difficult to create a common vision and at the same time to uphold personal interests as a priority, the liberal model is in crisis. Many congregations are experiencing this tension as they try to bring into focus a sense of mission and balance it with personal development and the commitment to community. They struggle to overcome apathy surrounding the building of community and indifference to world suffering.[10]

A new crossroads

It seems evident that religious congregations are at a crossroads. They can chose to function as priest or as magician before the reality of the Church and the world today. One choice involved in this decision is the willingness to come to terms with the creation of a common social vision, and to focus on the real needs of others, transcending personal interests and comfortable patterns.[11] It is the challenge of generativity.

If we as religious reject the challenge of generativity, some congregations may go the way of all "magical" communities and either attract only those who seek escape or simply disappear. We need to ask ourselves if it is our inability to allow religion to function in a transformative manner in our congregations which is calling into question the future of religious life. If this is so, the present malaise about our future is a crisis created by the mechanisms which can be changed. It is *not* one inherent to the meaning of religious life itself.

As in the life of an adult, the crisis of generativity in a religious congregation is a normal point of development. The healing effects of the post-Vatican II therapeutic style of religious life are important. There would be no development in religious life without them. However, the danger today is stagnation—remaining, as individuals and congregations, in a period of development long after our need for the supports of this style of life has been met.

The promise contained in facing a new call is that the self-identity gained through the helps of this period can be transformed into a stance of care and wisdom which mark the transformative

---

10. Gerald A. Arbuckle, "Suffocating Religious Life: A New Type Emerges," *The Way*, No. 65 (Summer 1989) 36.

11. Mary Jo Leddy, *op. cit.*, 41.

community. Care which overcomes the apathy of self-absorption ultimately reflects God's own care for the world and releases the transformative dimension of religion into everyday life.

Wisdom which can face the losses inherent in life's limits is a detached concern with life itself and its meaning. Such wisdom leads to responsible renunciation, the ability to let go in order to enter more deeply into an authentic response to reality.[12] However, the question which faces religious congregations today is what aspect of reality has the power to most deeply call us to life?

12. Margaret Farley, *Personal Commitments*, 111.

CHAPTER FIVE

Beyond the Liberal Model: The Capacity to Transform

Naming the shadow of an affluent culture

Religious life throughout the history of the Church has provided an alternative life style not only within the Church but also within society. Each age of religious life made its statement from within the culture from which it grew. The flight to the desert of the early monks was a critique of the deterioration of Roman civilization. The mendicant orders in the Middle Ages called into question the status of landed wealth and the societal paralysis of the feudal system. The teaching congregations of the 1800s critiqued the long-standing social practice that only the elite could be educated.

The call to follow Jesus Christ as a religious has always involved a concomitant social stance. The social stance expresses a practical consequence of Jesus'call at a particular time in history. The stance itself is not the call; rather, it represents a deeper response of the heart. It witnesses that something more than the normal motivations of life lies at the heart of this vocation. This motivation is strong enough to give one a new perspective, not only on one's own life but on society as well. The stance emphasizes that a religious vocation is not just for the religious alone, but is to have an effect on the condition of human life in their day.

What is the social stance that religious orders take today? In the face of our present global situation, what is the historical call which unmistakably recaptures the basic countercultural charism of religious life? This chapter discusses these questions and also the new realism which communities need in order to respond to this call today.

The focus today

There are many needs in the world today. However, one stands out to challenge religious as they enter a new millennium. Religious life is called today to witness that all of humanity has a relationship to the poor of the world. Denial of the presence of the poor and our responsibility to them is one of the major deceptions of our times. Such denial requires the clarity of a counter-response in order for the power of the denial to be overcome.

The denial of the poor functions in our society in the same manner as the denial of the shadow, or unclaimed aspects of personality, operates in each adult life. Through various mechanisms, people simply deny parts of their personality that do not fit into their operative self-image or the one confirmed by society.[1] This denial does not make the unwanted characteristics go away. It simply hides them from view.

In the same manner, the poor function as the shadow of an affluent society where many deny the existence of the poor. The poor remind us of the fact that not everyone wins or succeeds, even in a land of opportunity. On a world-wide level, their presence is even more disturbing. Global poverty is not an accident. The growing number of poor people in the world is a direct result of the post-war economic choices of first-world countries in liaison with the ruling elites of poor nations.[2] The fact remains that poverty is the result of behaviors which many people do not want to give up.

The national level is no better. There are more poor people in the United States today than there were ten years ago. This is the result of economic and political choices made in recent years. Since a consumer life style and persistent poverty are related, facing the poor as our shadow has to be a concern of each individual

1. William Miller, *Your Golden Shadow* (San Francisco: Harper & Row, 1989).

2. For a good overview of the relationship between first-world responsibility and world poverty, see: Elizabeth Morgan, Van B. Weigel, and Eric De-Baufre, *Global Poverty and Personal Responsibility: Integrity Through Commitment* (New York: Paulist Press, 1989).

and of every religious congregation.[3] However, the basic stance of many people of developed nations toward the poor is denial. Religious congregations can also share in this apathy.

Relationship to the poor

"Relationship to the poor" has a slightly different emphasis from the term "option for the poor" used in the Church today. It is a more fundamental stance which points to the fact that individuals and groups are related to the poor whether they make an option for them at a conscious level or not. In other words, persons not only create a relationship with the poor by being for them, but they are also judged by their relationship to the poor because they are integrally related to them in their humanity already. It is only a society addicted to a false definition of the meaning of life and its essential relationships which can deny this fact.

Religious are called to witness to an alternative posture in this social context. Owning a relationship to the poor is one way a congregation can communicate its religious inspiration. Why is this so? The poor are not affirmed by any prevailing system of wisdom. Response to them witnesses to the nature of true religion; that is, religion connects people with a meaning system which is more comprehensive than their culture's. This connection should illumine life's values in spite of the darkness of personal and societal blindness.

The social stance of religious congregations for the poor is not synonymous with the entire meaning of religious life. It is only one way that religious witness to the meaning of God in their lives. However, a care which transcends that of self-interest—on behalf of the poor—is an important symbol today. It witnesses that belief in God generates a care and vision beyond self-concern.

The challenge of the poor

Increasing numbers of poor people are a human reality which has no parallel in the world today in its seriousness. The poor stand

3. See, for example: the challenge presented in the Bishop's Economic Pastoral, "Economic Justice for All: Catholic Social Teaching and the U.S. Economy," *Origins: N.C. Documentary Service* 16 (November 27, 1986) 408–455.

in direct contradiction to all that the modern person professes to be valuable in modern life. They critique our world views by their very presence. Their suffering is not one which can be explained away or predicted as a normal stage of the life cycle. The narrative of their suffering challenges to the core the adequacy of the entire meaning-system of first-world society. For them, hard work and initiative do not bring prosperity. Rather, hard work brings more hard work, and initiative is stamped out by systems organized to keep them poor. The very meaning of human freedom is challenged when the experience of many in the world is that the material means to have options are not theirs.[4]

Religious people of the world have to examine the relationship between response to poverty and true religion. Is religion helping the world move forward as a community or is it providing another means for it to turn in on itself?[5] This question is a common one for the East and West, both for Christians and those of other faiths. The two largest groups of people today with whom believers are in dialogue are the poor and the nonbeliever. Religious congregations share in the witness of all religion before both groups as they discern their response to the world crisis of poverty today.

However, a religious community cannot contribute authentically to the formation of a public consensus to deal better with the concerns of the poor if their own internal life is simply a mirror of the problems of an affluent culture. Acknowledgment of a relationship to the poor requires ongoing change in religious congregations. The challenge of the poor today is deeper than a stated "option for the poor" that allows us to continue a destructive life style and provide aid to the needy. It precludes the support of a foreign policy that dictates crippling trade relationships, yet provides for minimal relief of debts so that the economic system does not collapse.[6] Rather, it is a decision for the poor which changes

4. Roger Haight raises the question, "What does it mean to say theologically that freedom defines human existence if so many human beings are in fact not free?" in *An Alternative Vision* (New York: Paulist Press, 1985) 34.

5. Aloysius Pieris, *An Asian Theology of Liberation* (New York: Orbis Books, 1988) 15–31.

6. J. Brian Hehir, "Third World Debt and the Poor," *Origins*, Vol. 18, 607–612.

people and groups while it transforms the situation. For religious, it is a decision focused not on the continuation of religious life as a therapeutic atmosphere, but on the health of a civilization which still has a chance to turn from the inevitable breakdown which will result from long-term denial.

The challenge facing religious today is to ask whether our corporate witness actually contributes to a new consciousness of the poor in our world. The countercultural message of religious life today has the power to touch the deepest pathology of our culture: that our common life in society requires more than a concern for material accumulation.[7]

Realism and corporate life

A congregation needs a new type of realism if it is going to witness corporately to the concerns of the poor and carry out its mission. In the remainder of this chapter, we are going to investigate the nature of this realism and why it is needed. We will also discuss the relationship between realism and the development of corporate life in a congregation today.

Corporate life is not easy to create. If a congregation wants a life together which is generative, that is, outward looking, and transformative, that is, creative and effective, the task is even greater. Probably one of the greatest enemies of a corporate life is romanticism.

Romanticism is a congregational environment which is focused primarily on feelings of compatibility or the internal dynamics of the group. When romanticism colors the response of a congregation to the society at large, a group can divert so much energy to differences among themselves that they isolate themselves from wider institutional networks which are essential for effectiveness.

Groups withdraw into outmoded institutional forms, clinging to past glory and waiting for the world to provide them with a context for mission which requires little change on their part. Or they stagnate because their over-critical and unrealistic expectations paralyze any constructive efforts in the congregation. In a romantic atmosphere, the false hope that someday the right person or the right

7. On this pathology in American culture, see: Robert Bellah, *Habits of the Heart*, 295.

project or the absence of external limitations will change everything is maintained. A magical or romantic approach to the stress of transition has to be offset by a realism which can face the limits and possibilities in the present situation.

A magical or romantic stance by a congregation can be reflected in many ways. Common ones are sectarianism and the maintenance of dysfunctional relational styles. Sectarianism forsakes constructive networking with others. In a sectarian atmosphere, people associate only with those who share their priorities and world view, and those who are perceived not to share the same outlook are never accepted as partners in a project or activity.

A great deal of energy is expended on clarifying who are insiders and who are outsiders in a sectarian atmosphere. Rigid boundaries are maintained between groups. Sectarianism is romantic because it focuses on the inner life of the group in an excessive manner. It makes behavioral or ideological conformity a higher value than networking with others in order to meet the needs of the wider society.[8] A sectarian outlook denies that bonding with others requires the acceptance of limitations and imperfection in order to achieve common goals. It is built on the premise that differences eliminate the possibility of a common effort.

A romantic or inward-looking stance is maintained in a congregation through support of dysfunctional behaviors and relationships in a community. The efforts to bond, which build a corporate life, are frustrated when this occurs. While the bad effects of certain ways of living are observed by members, nothing is done to change them.

Nesting is one type of romantic and dysfunctional behavior. Nesting is the refusal to be apostolically mobile. Personal needs offset the responsibility to move when ministerial effectiveness is gone or when needs have been met. A romantic environment is strengthened through nesting because ministerial energy is transformed into keeping a job so that life can go on as usual.

Allowing dysfunctional relational styles to influence a community's life has negative results. However, this is often denied by community members. The needs of the community or of mission

8. Robert K. Merton, "The Perspectives of Insiders and Outsiders" in *The Sociology of Science: Theoretical and Empirical Investigations* (Chicago: The University of Chicago Press, 1973) 99–136.

are overlooked because it is easier to accept than to confront addictive and dysfunctional behaviors.

Activity and passivity

What type of realism is needed in a group in order for it to be generative? First, a realistic vision of the role of activity and passivity in the group's relationships is helpful. Since the advent of social analysis, groups have had a more refined ability to analyze the structural relationships which create certain problems in society and in the Church. However, along with this skill has come the illusion that the ability to analyze a situation gives the group immediate control over it.

This illusion leads to frustration and hostility within the group when the action plans which stem from analysis do not bring changes in structures as quickly as changes in insight were achieved.[9] What is often overlooked in these analyses is the role of culture in changing the situation. Cultural change takes time, and when this fact is ignored, political or economic changes are short lived. The same applies to changing Church structures. Religious congregations committed to the renewal of the Church have to be committed to change not only in the short term, but also in the long run.

A congregation with a realistic balance between activity and passivity can assess its options for growth and effectiveness by evaluating its present situation and its potential for change. Every group is limited by its place in society, its present group consciousness, its cultural make-up, and its environment. This is the passive or received dimension of the group's life. It is always a given. While its shape can be altered, it is never erased.

Without these limits, however, the group would not have an identity. A group can feel limited by its association with a hierarchical Church, immersion in a consumer society, citizenship in a particular country, or a limitation in the background of its membership. However, it cannot exist without some type of limits. These limits simply reveal the incarnational character of the group's life. Its members cannot develop without these structures, even

9. Francisco F. Claver, S.J., "Cultural Analysis Toward Social Change," *Pulso*, Vol. 1, No. 1 (Manila: 1984) 48–63.

in their imperfection. This is the condition of being situated. However, it is also a condition which can be changed.

Healthy groups assess their potential for change and set realistic goals to transform their limits, rather than dissociate from them. However, a congregation changes only if a sufficient number of its members are active within it. Unlike the romantic view which holds that change will occur through some magical consensus or lack of external constraint, a realistic outlook sees that change occurs from the inside, through the involvement of people in the institution.

Owning its potential for healthy interaction and change is critical in a religious congregation. The tensions of maintaining relationships with formal Church structures, developing ministries, and responding to economic and political realities are difficult. Putting aside a romantic outlook and facing these issues with realism gives a group a corporate life which is generative, and a new future.

Facing situations of injustice

A second way a congregation needs to act with realism is by naming the situations of injustice in its midst. All congregational relationships bring with them limitations, or a repression of possibilities. One city manager puts it this way: "A group can do many things, but it cannot do everything." However, sometimes the limitations generated by choices or relationships are unnecessary. Involvement in a particular ministry, culture, diocese, or nation can bring injustice, not the normal limitation which accompanies choice or relationship. These injustices are generated not by the needs of human association but from the additional interests of domination.

There are various types of unjust relationships. Some situations of injustice are within the congregation. Others are between the congregation and outside groups. A third type occurs within the congregation's own ministerial relationships. No group can address all of these problems.

It is essential for congregations to prioritize which situations of injustice they will address. The question to be asked is whether a community is part of effective solutions to problems outside itself. If romanticism prevails, a group will not generate this question. The group vision will be limited to the pursuit of self-interest as long as members do not infringe on one another. Responsibility to others, which is basic to the right to exist as a congregation in the Church, will not seem important. However, realism within a congregation poses this hard question: Does its lifestyle produce an effective mission?

When congregations lack this realism, they can also sink into romantic behaviors regarding their own problems. They can take for granted their social environment the same way people can ignore responsibilities to restore natural resources. For instance, religious can expect their congregation, like nature, to simply replenish itself. They can be so caught up in their own interests that the adult responsibility it takes to maintain their corporate life is ignored. Members can rely on a shared past or present personal relationships alone, without addressing the transformations and common vision needed to have a shared future.[10]

The result of denial is visible on a natural plane in the destruction of resources in our world. On a group or social level, the damage is more subtle. Denial leads to the erosion of the "social ecology" of group life. Social ecology is the web of moral understandings and commitments that tie people together in community.[11]

When the problems which lead to the collapse of common understandings are left unaddressed and new understandings are not made explicit, people lose faith in the bonds of trust which once held them together. The result is fear, apathy, or withdrawal. These sentiments are expressed on a group level in stagnation or the rejection of the challenge to be generative.

Developing a generative focus

A group takes a generative stance when it assumes the responsibility to direct its life and shape the environment in which it lives. This requires a third type of realism, a generative focus. Realism demands that a congregation focus its energies. Priorities have to be set and effective responses to situations of injustice have to be searched out.

10. Mary Jo Leddy, "Beyond the Liberal Model," 46.
11. Robert Bellah, *Habits of the Heart*, 335.

A congregation can work at this task in two general ways. It can assess how its charism gives direction to the group's response. If this approach is adopted, the focus will arise from the vision of spirituality it employs to meet situations in the Church and society. A group may need to update its understanding of its spirituality. This is different from an historical study of charism. In this case, the congregation uses social analysis to understand its world and then asks the significance of its charism for its response. Through this new medium it can uncover the potential of its charism for guiding decisions.

For instance, a congregation whose charism involves expressing the providence of God may use this vision to discern how to use its limited personnel in a local church to care for the homeless. The community in this instance has certain intentions in acting that distinguish them as a group.[12]

This focus on normative beliefs within the group which characterize them as a group is a study of its character. Just as knowing an individual's character can give insight into how he or she will behave in a situation, a group character can give similiar direction. The community identifies its character by those beliefs which they want to influence their concrete choices as a congregation. They intend that certain traits will characterize them, whatever activity they take on as a group. This provides a certain consistency and self-understanding in the manner in which they carry out their ministry.

A congregation can also take another approach to setting a generative focus. It can periodically set corporate priorities, situations of injustice which will be areas of corporate commitment. This approach focuses less on the character of the congregation's charism and more on a common praxis, or action, aimed at changing situations and the participants. Just as parents take on the generative task of their adulthood by raising their children, a congregation can move toward a generative atmosphere through intentionally taking on tasks and corporate relationships as a group.

---

12. An understanding of character is developed by Stanley Hauerwas in "Toward an Ethics of Character," *Introduction to Christian Ethics*, ed. by Ronald P. Hamel and Kenneth R. Himes, O.F.M. (New York: Paulist Press, 1989) 151–162.

Corporate commitments make visible a congregational mission. While many groups cannot maintain the commitments they once did, some are still necessary. Corporate commitments narrow options and offer a different type of common experience from institutional commitments alone. However, former institutional commitments can be reinterpreted in light of a new understanding of a corporate focus. For instance, a congregation may have a high school in a geographical area targeted for focused ministry effort. This traditional ministry could be redefined as part of a larger ministry which may include day care, community development, and social service assistance.

Selected corporate commitments can provide experiences around which members can bond and interpret their ministry. By acting together and reflecting on that action in light of the gospel, a group can get insight into the identity of their charism as it impacts this issue or this situation.

Instead of focusing on character directly, a generative focus is expressed through mission to a local church. The priorities set can be common projects or issues which the group chooses as foci. This type of focus can evoke a commitment which requires members to contribute to the fulfillment of a common project. It can give them some insight into the impact of their common effort and distinctive spirituality. The experience of a common action gives a new focus to the group.

Setting corporate commitments allows the group to meet a ministry situation on grounds other than what the situation itself provides. Instead of their response being grounded primarily in their sense of character, it is grounded in a corporate intention to shape the situation in a new way through various types of concrete action. Either or both of these methods can serve to develop a generative focus as part of the realism needed for corporate life today.

Three models of generative response

There are three general types of situations of injustice which can focus a sense of charism for a congregation. Priorities can be set by asking which type of situation can be effectively met by a group. The types are minimum needs, enhancement needs, and criticism of ideology.

MINIMUM NEEDS

These needs concern the acquisition of the *minimum* needed for human life. People can change their life situation only when the primary conditions for food, clothing, and shelter and the proper means for insuring their use and maintenance have been met. To deny another this minimum is to deny what is essential for a basic human life or for the operation of their freedom. A congregation could adopt such a focus to oppose whatever creates this lack of necessities and to work to provide the conditions where all can have access to the minimum needed for life and growth. This could be further specified in terms of housing, hunger, or medical needs. A congregation could reexamine its charism specifically in terms of its relevance for meeting these repressions at the level of the minimum needed for human life.

ENHANCEMENT NEEDS

Another type of situation of injustice exists at the level of what is needed for the enhancement of human life. Human freedom is not just oriented toward survival but toward development. However, people often lack the means to build the world of the future.[13] They experience a type of repression which denies them the means for the building of culture: the generation of life, the means for education, freedom of opinion and worship, opportunities to work, and equality of sex, race, and nation. A congregation could focus both on the opposition to movements which block these relationships and also on the construction of situations which promote them. It could ask itself what message its charism brings to the resolution of these oppressions.

CRITICISM OF IDEOLOGY

A third type of situation of injustice is repression at the level of ideology. Ideology is a complex of values and behavior patterns communicated by a society to an individual, which are prejudiced in favor of the vested interests within the society.[14] Ideology is often

13. Denis Goulet, *The Cruel Choice: A New Concept in the Theory of Development* (New York: Atheaneum, 1977).

14. For a discussion of ideology, see: *Theology and Sociology: A Reader*, ed. and intro. by Robin Gill (New York: Paulist Press, 1987) 79ff., 138ff.

experienced as the common explanation in a culture of why things are the way they are. Ideology explains why people are poor, why women should not be managers, why it is alright to have racially separate schools. Ideology has to be criticized to the degree it blocks social change, or gives good excuses for ignoring the needs of those who are marginated.

Congregations which take as their focus the question of ideology will invest much energy in works such as religious education, support of groups suffering the destruction of their culture, women's issues, and political action. Groups can find new meanings in their charism by posing its relevance to transforming current ideologies such as patriarchy, materialism, nihilism, and determinism.

When a group sets a generative focus, it may focus on one or several of these types of situations. A general mission focus such as sharing in the liberating work of Jesus Christ in the Church could be enhanced by specific goals in each of these areas.

A generative focus is an aspect of the realism needed in corporate life today because it provides a communal focus in meeting needs beyond the group. It builds concrete ways in which the congregation is going to contribute to the Church and society by discerning what cannot be effectively addressed and what must be changed. It can mark why and how they will subordinate personal interests in order to participate in a broader network of care. This decision does not need to be for an indefinite period, but can be for a specific time, for instance, from chapter to chapter.

Decisions made for a generative focus can help to sustain a congregation in their identity through ongoing corporate investment. The communal processes involved in setting such a focus can give members ownership of a stance which is larger than their interpersonal relationships. The process can engage the members in a cultural critique that acknowledges not all social limits are good, yet some limits are necessary.

CHAPTER SIX

Signposts on the Journey:
The Search for Wisdom

Not all experience since renewal is worthy of reflecting on for
the future. Holding onto past hurts, focusing on what was negative in pre-Vatican religious life, or idealizing the past in selective
memory are all experiences that can prove to be useless as sources
of light for forward movement.

The type of experience which can be a source of direction for
ongoing renewal, is that which raises issues of the meaning of religious life in the Church. In other words, experiences which lead
religious to rethink the large questions of meaning and which help
them to correct previous understandings of their relationship to
God and one another are the real signposts on the journey of
renewal.

This stage in the journey of religious life for those who have
been active in renewal since the council can be characterized in part
as the struggle between melancholy and wisdom in their lives as
congregations. There have been a lot of changes since the council,
but there have also been many losses. Loss of large institutions,
loss of a sense of a unified and commonly accepted way of living,
loss of signs of the prosperity of the congregations, loss of members through death and departure, and loss of the hopeful sign of
many members coming to join or take over the ministries, weigh
on many members. These losses can easily contribute to a sense
of melancholy.

Melancholy differs from the normal mourning that these losses
would entail. Mourning is a natural process by which a person ac-

knowledges the sadness caused by separation from loved ones, projects in which he or she has invested, and powers or abilities once possessed. In mourning, a person gradually withdraws interest and investment in lost relationships and projects, at least in the same manner in which they were once held. At the same time, the person transforms his or her relationship to them.

While one accepts the loss of these loved people and things and continues to remember their presence, he or she learns from these losses a lesson about the whole of life. Life involves renunciation, even the loss of dimensions of life which seemed at one time so essential to personal vitality. Mourning helps a person or group to let go and open themselves in hope to the next stage of the mystery of life both as individuals and as congregations.

Melancholy, on the other hand, in the spiritual tradition has been associated with rancor or anger.[1] When someone gives in to the feelings of melancholy, he or she refuses to accept the loss of someone or something loved and instead is filled with resentment. A person wants to avenge his or her loss. When the futility of this effort becomes apparent, rage is often turned inward or against those associated with the diminishment. Cloaked anger and unconscious hostility infiltrate relationships. A person adopts a despairing attitude toward life and gives up all but the most trivial desires. In fact, melancholy is a radical form of self-preoccupation, where a person not only abandons the pursuit of substantial values, as in apathy, but declares these pursuits were never really worth the effort in the first place.

Melancholy robs a person of the capacity to look back on his or her personal or congregational life with a sense of order, meaning and coherence, or a sense of integrity. The capacity to think is weakened because it is filled with resentment. In this way, melancholy creates a blindness far deeper than physical blindness.[2]

The result is a person who can no longer affirm. One can only denounce and repudiate. Unlike mourning, melancholy cannot transcend loss to discover a more universal meaning in which to find new ways of loving. This includes a new and different kind of love for significant people, for those of other generations, for

1. St. Gregory the Great, *Pastoral Care*, trans. by Henry Davis. *The Ancient Christian Writers*, No. 11 (New York: Newman Press, 1950).

2. Donald Capps, *Deadly Sins and Saving Virtues, op. cit.*, 63–70, 110–116.

new ways of living, and for oneself as a "good enough" person who has faced the successes and failures of a particular life cycle.

Wisdom is the quality which assists individuals and groups in this battle with melancholy. It is the capacity to view life and human problems from the perspective of the meaning of life as a whole. It involves a detached concern from human problems. Often wisdom is associated with the virtue of aging. It is an outlook on life which looks for solutions to human problems not from the perspective of self-interest but rather from that of ultimate concerns. Wisdom is also a response to loss. Instead of responding to loss with the disgust and self-absorption of melancholy, wisdom seeks to find in the loss the key to life's meanings which lay buried in it.

Wisdom continues its care for the next generation by living in a manner which reflects the consolidation of life's true meanings. In its rejection of melancholy, wisdom witnesses that there is more to life than yielding to the temptation to feel passed over and forgotten. Wisdom is not a posture of pronouncing edicts on the meaning of life. Rather, it is a quality of living which acts on the essential meanings of life as daily practice. In face of loss, or age, or transition, wisdom holds firm, with a sense of peace and wholeness, to what really matters. In contrast to the melancholic posture of being at odds with self and at odds with life, wisdom communicates to the next generation that fidelity to a way of life with its losses and successes is possible and is inherent to life's meaning.

Discovering our own wisdom

When the Church asked religious congregations to delve into the primitive experience of their charism, it asked them to tap their collective wisdom in order to face the massive transitions before them today. Congregations were not to pine over past times of highly visible institutions, large numbers, and uniformity of life. Rather, they were to dig deep into the meaning of their lives and discover a center of integrity which could lead them into their next stage of life as a group.

The creation of the center needed by individual religious and by congregations for movement into the future is based on two general beliefs or principles held by their shared tradition. The first is the affirmation that the charism and traditions of congregations within the tradition of the Church are not bankrupt. In affirming this belief, the congregation rejects melancholy. The second is the belief that one's personal story and the communal story of renewal find their true meaning only within the larger story of Jesus of Nazareth. This is a posture of wisdom.

There are certain truths of life that the enormous transitions which we experience today do not erase. Religious belong to a community of people who have chosen to find their identity and meaning within the single concrete story of Jesus of Nazareth. They believe that within those limits they meet God. They can make choices among the many voices in their lives because, in Jesus, they find the central paradigm showing that limits can lead to fullness and growth. Thus they affirm the paschal mystery and the primary focus of their personal and communal commitment. This is a stance centered in faith. It is a gift of grace and the source of their freedom to create their lives and the direction of religious life in the future.

Even the idea of affirmation of the person, which has been so central to renewal for many congregations, can be clarified by this essential stance. A movement into the future, from a therapeutic community to a transformative one, need not mean an abandonment of respect for the person. Rather, the journey of the last thirty years can give a new vision into the meaning of the person that religious life is committed to uphold.

Religious life can have a center. Even though the notion of the person which has emerged since renewal has been shaped by many sources and experiences, it can be integrated into a new vision of religious life. This center can be expressed by beliefs about what it means to be a full human being as a religious. These beliefs can be signposts as religious make choices for the future.

Beliefs need not just be statements or ideals. They are meant to function, in the shaping of congregations, as signs along the journey. When our beliefs are centered in experience and flow from personal and communal synthesis, they can direct future choice.[3] They are a "wisdom" needed for the next stage of the journey.

3. For a helpful discussion of the role of personal and communal history in discernment, see: John English, *Choosing Life* (New York: Paulist Press, 1978).

Perhaps wisdom in its deepest theological sense is a consensus about what is ultimately believed about life, and how these beliefs affect choices in a group. This consensus can lead a group to reach out to certain choices and to eliminate others. These beliefs function as statements of collective wisdom to guide decision making. As principles, they contain the moral wisdom acquired through experience. Let us look at some principles of renewal that can guide ongoing decision making both by individuals and congregations, although these principles will be discussed at more length in subsequent chapters of this book.

PEOPLE ARE NOT PURE SPIRITS. THEY ARE INDIVIDUALS WITH STRENGTHS AND WEAKNESSES, BODIES AND SOULS.[4] Religious have owned that personal and spiritual development cannot be done in abstraction from past histories, cultures, human potentials, or weaknesses. Entering religious life is not like lifting the page on a magic slate in which one's past, sexuality, interests, or personal strengths and weaknesses are erased so that spiritual development can be written afresh.[5]

RELIGIOUS HAVE NOT LEFT THE WORLD. A person who comes to religious life today cannot move into a life situation removed from his or her culture. The separation from the world called for in the council's understanding of religious life is a subtlety of discernment in living and a clarity of public witness.[6]

PERSONAL HOLINESS INVOLVES CONTEMPLATION IN ACTION, WHERE THE WORLD IS A SOURCE OF REVELATION.[7] The world is not viewed as a distraction from the spiri-

4. The use of the term "soul" here is not technical. It refers simply to the transcendent dimension of an embodied human life. It does not suggest the dualism of body and soul criticized in much literature today.

5. For a more technical treatment of this subject, see: Karl Rahner, "Concerning the Relationship between Nature and Grace," *Theological Investigations* I (Baltimore: Helicon, 1963) 297–318.

6. On the notion of separation, see: Sharon Holland, "Religious and Secular Consecration in the Code," *Seminarium* 23 (October–December, 1983) 519–528.

7. Karl Rahner, "Theology of Freedom," *Theological Investigations* II (Baltimore: Helicon, 1963) 178–196. For a feminist interpretation of this essential understanding, see: Elizabeth Schussler Fiorenza, "Feminist Spirituality, Christian Identity and Catholic Vision" in *Womanspirit Rising*. Ed. by Carol P. Christ and Judith Plaskow (New York: Harper & Row, 1979) 146.

tual life, rather a locus in which all can be hearers of the Word of God.

THE FULFILLMENT OF A RELIGIOUS AND HIS OR HER MINISTRY INVOLVES A REALISTIC KNOWLEDGE OF THE WORLD THAT INVOLVES HUMAN VALUES AND TECHNICAL KNOWLEDGE.[8] This fulfillment demands that individuals and groups have the capacity to integrate a vision of what is truly human with the skills needed to be effective.

PERSONS NEED TO BE ENGAGED IN MEANINGFUL WORK THAT CONTRIBUTES TO THE WIDER COMMUNITY AND GIVES THE INDIVIDUALS A SENSE THAT THERE IS A CONGRUENCE BETWEEN THEIR GIFTS AND THE MINISTRY. Religious recognize the benefits of respecting individual gifts in the choice of ministry. This is not selfishness but an aspect of respect for persons.

MINISTRY IS MORE THAN DOING WORKS AND FULFILLING A FUNCTION OR PLUGGING A HOLE. Freud says the ability to love and work marks the mature person. Theologians say *work* proceeds from the divine vocation to be human which involves going out of self. In contrast, *works* are simply things done. When people do not have this deeper sense of work, consumerism and addiction in its many forms can occur.

FREEDOM ONLY COMES TO FULFILLMENT WITHIN COMMUNITY. Religious today know that inherent to the meaning of freedom is the bonding or integration of the achievements of all. Development of healthy relationships is key to this. They are not only persons in ministry, they are communities in ministry.

WORK IS TO CONTRIBUTE TO THE ONGOING TRANSFORMATION OF THE QUALITY OF LIFE FOR ALL PEOPLE, ESPECIALLY THE POOR. The work of religious congregations must be continually expansive and more universal, reaching people who are on the fringe of present services, those marginated in any way, especially the materially poor.

THERE MUST BE ACCOUNTABILITY FOR TIME AND ENERGIES BECAUSE THE CALL TO BE PERSONS INVOLVES THE CALL TO BE EFFECTIVE. The charism of religious in the Church must be linked and adapted to specific people

8. Juan Luis Segundo, *Faith and Ideologies, op. cit.,* 90ff.

and concrete places.[9] This calls a community to change and ongoing critical reflection.

COMMUNITY IS NOT JUXTAPOSING ALREADY-FINISHED INDIVIDUALS. Community is not only something formed by mutual consent. Community is a system of human reactions and interrelationships which form part of the human condition of all.[10] We understand the fact that community is essential to life at times through the negative experience of the pain of its absence.

PERSONS CANNOT DEVELOP WITHOUT DEVELOPING COMMUNITY AND SOCIETY. This offsets the popular belief that one comes to freedom as if in a cupboard and bounces out to interact with others only when he or she chooses. Community is not a support group which meets once a week; rather, it is a life group which forms an integral part of personal development.

TO PROMOTE THE DEVELOPMENT OF PERSONS, HUMAN RELATIONSHIPS WHICH ARE DEHUMANIZING HAVE TO BE CHANGED THROUGH THE CHANGING OF INSTITUTIONS WHICH PERPETUATE AND STRUCTURE THESE RELATIONSHIPS. Religious have found that just as they must change the "givens" in their personality and histories as part of personal and religious development, so also they are to change structures and ways of relating.

AN ONGOING TASK OF BEING A PERSON IS TO EXAMINE THE SPOKEN AND UNSPOKEN RULES WHICH GUIDE US TO SEE IF THEY ARE PRODUCTIVE FOR THE TOTALITY OF VALUES WHICH COMPRISE OUR LIVES. Religious have spent years examining their beliefs. Is the sister wearing the work apron always the most generous? Is the brother always at home the most community minded? Have changed structures really freed religious for ministry and a deeper sense of

9. For aspects of this challenge, see: John Coleman, *An American Strategic Theology* (New York: Paulist Press, 1982). Elizabeth Schussler Fiorenza, "Feminist Theology as a Critical Theology of Liberation" in *Woman: New Directions*, ed. by Walter Burkhardt (New York: Paulist Press, 1977) 29–50. Carl Starkloff, "Ideology and Mission Spirituality" in *Review for Religious*, Vol. 45, No. 4 (July/August, 1986) 554–566.

10. Juan Luis Segundo, *Grace and the Human Condition, op. cit.*, 26, 37.

community? This type of questioning is essential to ongoing renewal.

The "more" calling us forward

Persons learn values by looking at a bigger picture. It is only before a view of life which is larger than the individual that anyone finds the direction and the motivation to do this. The decision of religious congregations to place emphasis on persons and the incorporation of all the means to do this can seem like fragmentation unless it is related to some deeper vision. The losses sustained over the last years can easily lead to melancholy unless individuals and congregations reclaim a sense of life larger than themselves. By vows, religious have affirmed another belief about the person, a belief which has the potential to address the problem of fragmentation in a radical way.

Mediation and the road to wisdom

WE BELIEVE IN MEDIATION. If one thought he or she could know, love, and serve God better without the community and the Church, that religious would not have made vows. Somehow, however vaguely, when we make vows, we state that our congregation will be the mediator in this highly personal commitment.

It is with these companions and following this way of life that we cast our lot in making a primary commitment to God. Each person says, indirectly, that in these limits he or she will find fullness of life. By making vows, religious state that the community and the Church are stable and permanent mediations in the midst of many others in their lives.

Personal life is a mediated life. All persons need stable communities of meaning in their lives to help them sort through the possibilities before them and bring them into a unified whole. The needs of a family, for example, channel the energies and focus the choices of many people.

Religious also need stable communities of meaning, mediations such as their congregations and the Church, to receive their gifts and to pull them out of themselves to reach out to possibilities they would not see on their own. The Church and the congregation cannot take responsibility for the lives of religious, nor are these mediations perfect, because they are concrete and human. Yet without them, religious will never come to true freedom or personal fulfillment or be able to measure the contribution of their lives.

These beliefs are not abstractions, but reflect the experience of many religious since renewal. As beliefs, they call into question the liberal model of religious life. Why is this so? A focus on the individual without emphasis on the commonly held values of the group, or a shared vision, cannot channel individual choice. Hence the liberal model alone is incapable of sustaining religious life as a vocation in the Church. It is our deeper beliefs as religious which point to the need for a new consensus about the meaning of our lives as religious congregations. The ongoing formation of this consensus is part of the mediating task of each community.

PART THREE

Rethinking the Vows

CHAPTER SEVEN

A New Stance on the Road

The life of the vows is a central symbol of religious life. The vows symbolize that religious life is a vocation; that is, the individuals who enter into it do not create the terms and conditions of their commitment entirely by their own will.[1] Understanding of the vows has shifted throughout the history of the Church.[2] Today, as in the past, rediscovering the meaning of the vows is an essential part of rethinking the foundations of religious life.

As they take up this task, religious find themselves in the position of travelers who, at an important juncture of their journey, get out their map to see where they've been and where they are going. The fact that this needs to be done is symbolic of the whole movement in religious life since the council.

Thirty years ago a map would not have been needed. Most religious assumed that they already knew the way. At that time the meaning of religious life was clearly articulated in an intricate system of rules and communal expectations. The challenge was not to search out the meaning of the vows, rather it was to be faithful to prescribed ways of living which promoted growth in their practice. Since the Second Vatican Council, religious have a deeper understanding that they, too, have to search in faith, as does each

---

1. James P. Hannigan, *Homosexuality: The Test Case For Christian Sexual Ethics, op. cit.,* 89, 106 n. 6.
2. See, for example, the study by John Lozano, *Life as a Parable: Reinterpreting the Religious Life* (New York: Paulist Press, 1986).

Christian man and woman of good will, to constantly redefine the meaning of their particular life stance in a changing world.

This awareness on the part of religious—as well as a change in their self-understanding—was stimulated by a parallel cultural shift in society. Teilhard de Chardin describes humankind as being like travelers on a boat.[3] Before the great advances of modern science, the concerns of people on this boat were basically directed toward managing its internal workings. They needed to know what made the ship run, how to interact down in the hold, how to organize themselves.

One day, however, someone climbed up on deck. This new experience shifted the human consciousness on the boat. People not only realized they could keep the boat running but they could also steer its course. They were no longer passive observers in the world, trying to learn its laws and live in harmony with it. They could also direct and change the world. People discovered that even nature could be changed by their own inventions.

Called to a new consciousness

In some ways, Chardin's image characterizes the movement in religious life since the council. Religious today approach the vows with a new consciousness. They have less confidence that the minute explanations given in the pre-conciliar Church exhaust their meaning. From the experience of a more active role in forming their own self-definition as congregations in the Church, they are asking new questions. They feel responsible to reexamine not only the structures and ways of living in religious life but also its central symbols.

Religious stand with other contemporary adults in their capacity to restructure central life-systems. They do so within perimeters which reflect essential truths of human life and religious experience. Hence, along with this new consciousness is the reciprocal responsibility to acknowledge the limits of redefinition. There is a kernel of meaning in religious life that is not elastic. Its destruction would mean not the transformation of religious life but its demise.

3. Pierre Teilhard de Chardin, *The Phenomenon of Man*, trans. by Bernard Wall (London: William Collins and Company, 1959).

Challenges in the interpretation of the vows

The shift in human consciousness expressed by Chardin did not simply provide people with a greater sense of personal responsibility; it also provided a new context for thinking about God, the world, and themselves. This new context is shared today by religious as they invest in new stances in their renewal.

In order for congregations to move from being receivers of a tradition to being creators of a new interpretation, they must understand the values of the tradition. This understanding will give them freedom to transform its symbols. Congregations are called today to take a creative role in this period of transition in the Church. One basis of this transformation is recognition of the developments in theology and the culture with which religious life must integrate. In this chapter, we will explore these developments.

If we examine the general understanding of the vows before the council, we will see that they were based on different notions of the person, God, and the world than are drawn upon in Vatican II theology. Previous approaches emphasized religious life as a higher vocation through which a person left the world in order to live his or her life in a more perfect way.

Before the council, religious life and the Christian life in general shared certain characteristics. Many scholars find this period marked by a spirit of minimalism, legalism, extrinsicism, and juridicism.[4] The first challenge in the theology of the vows is to transcend the limits of this interpretative framework, to incorporate its strengths, and then to move beyond its limitations. Examining each of the tendencies can indicate the direction of this movement.

Minimalism approaches the practice of the vows in terms of minimum standards and requirements. For example, the meaning of celibacy could be eclipsed under the minimal notion of abstinence. With Vatican II, minimalism is not dead in religious life; rather, it has a liberal face. When communities simply do together the minimum and view their lifestyle as indistinguishable from cultural trends, minimalism is alive and well. Hence, moving an understanding of the vows beyond minimalism remains a problem in religious life today.

4. Timothy O'Connell, *Principles for a Catholic Morality, op. cit.*, chapter 2.

Legalism is an undue focus on the law, which reduces the vowed life to the letter of the law. It overemphasizes fidelity to minute customs as a measure of faithfulness. In a liberal life style, legalism still is a motivator. We see it in the tendency to use permission of the central authority as legitimation for what is right and wrong, without personal scrutiny of what values are at stake. In an atmosphere tolerant of a wide variety of life styles and ministries, this new legalism can have the same crippling effects on the moral development of the religious as the old legalism had.

Extrinsicism is the practice of judging an act only by the nature of the act, without consideration of the circumstances and intention surrounding the act. An external comformity which eliminated personal discretion in decision making had a major place in pre-Vatican life. Extrinsicism in the post-Vatican community is more subtle. It appears as an adherence to various ideological stances which substitute for serious discernment.

If a person says, I am a conservative, I am a feminist, I am for justice, I belong to a particular psychological school of thought, and then identifies so strongly with this stance that no new information can be absorbed, that person is stuck in an ideological stance. When this occurs, the meaning of religious life or the Christian life is reduced to a single focus through which an individual or group tries to interpret all problems.

Usually, ideological conformity is stimulated by the same addiction to superficial bonding as the old extrinsicism. Those elements of community expectations, Church life or Christian tradition which cannot be easily integrated with the prevailing single focus are either reinterpreted or pushed to the margin. The new extrinsicism is appealing because it responds to the anxiety generated by rapid change. It transports individuals from the darkness of faith to the false light of some sense of community which is brought about by ideological certitude.

Finally, juridicism is an undue emphasis on the role of law in the moral life. We recognize the motto, "Keep the rule and the rule will keep you" as an operative principle in many religious congregations. This in itself can be good. Over-emphasis on the law, however, can lead to an abandonment of its spirit. Then the law no longer serves the call to conversion inherent in the vowed life.

The new juridicism of post-Vatican community life is evident in the juridical spirit some religious display toward the new laws they have internalized from the secular culture. This could be the law of individualism or professionalism or "you do your thing and I'll do mine and we will agree not to question each other." These laws can figure just as rigidly in post-Vatican community life and serve the same purpose as pre-Vatican juridicism. They permit a mechanical bonding which evades the shared life which is implied in the life of the vows.

General developments in the theology of the vows

A transformed view of the vows can move beyond these categories by incorporating some of the following developments. A primary change of focus in the theology of the vows is the effort *to overcome a split between what is supernatural and what is natural*. It was thought in the past that one needed to leave the world, which was natural, in order to pay adequate attention to the concerns of the Christian life, which were supernatural. Religious were encouraged to adopt a supernatural life by rising above natural tendencies. This type of focus on the supernatural life fostered a split between what was supernatural and natural, and implied that only the supernatural was valuable. Furthermore, it could excuse one from grappling with the real problems of human life.[5]

In post-Vatican life, a split between what is natural and supernatural still exists. Religious congregations can promote a spirit of faith which is simply a reflection of secular faith. That is, it has no factor which distinguishes it from life in the secular culture. When this occurs, religious life is still detached from worldly existence, not by its physical separation, but by its moral detachment. Religious values have no significant influence on concrete choice. As congregations struggle to identify with their culture and still be countercultural in it, this tension is resolved.

Another development is a change in emphasis from fidelity to duties to a *sense of personal responsibility*. Fidelity in religious life includes adherence to duties, but also involves much more. Adherence to duties alone is a very limited view of the responsibility of a religious. Today, we see the vowed life as a process by which a

5. The theology of the "two planes" is discussed at length in Gustavo Gutierrez, *A Theology of Liberation*, trans. by Sister Caridad Inda and John Eagleson (New York: Orbis Books, 1973).

man or woman becomes fully human and enters creatively into the same challenge to transform the world as other adults. A life of the vows increases rather than diminishes responsibility, just as any life stance does.

Overemphasis on duties can continue in religious congregations when the life of the vows is reduced to a life of mission only. No one wants to live in an atmosphere where the common life is experienced only as a life of function, yet religious frequently create such climates. Such a community atmosphere eclipses the deeper meaning of religious life. A workaholic climate creeps into everyday life to such an extent that relationships suffer. Work, while it appears to reflect a strong commitment, can be an escape from the responsibility to relate to others in meaningful ways. Work is easier than investment in the tensions and integrity of relationships which require suffering and abandonment of self.

To emphasize personal responsibility, however, is not to dismiss obedience as childish. Today, the vow of obedience is a means to develop as an adult. All adults appeal to authority, obey authority, and are in authority at some time. Structures of obedience in the religious community such as communal discernment, congregational processes, and roles of authority call the religious to both obey authority and participate in authority. Both responses of the vow of obedience require a sense of personal responsibility which is accountable to others and to values beyond oneself.

We see personal responsibility today as marked by the ability to listen to God, others, and reality as they enter into life. Since its fruits are a stronger ability to love, this type of personal responsibility is the basis for a vowed commitment. Religious can continue today to interpret the vow of obedience in an adult framework through taking responsibility for their lives and congregations.

A fourth development in the theology of the vows is recognition of the *universal call of all Christians to holiness*. Discipleship, conversion, covenantal relationship with God, are not only applicable to religious life but to the lives of all Christians. Religious live in co-discipleship with others, not in a relationship of superiority to them.

An air of superiority can continue if religious expect to be exempted from the shared life of all people in the Church. Fidelity to a pilgrim church requires a certain amount of suffering today.

Married people struggle with personal decisions amid the controversy over birth control. Single people work with parish structures which still regard them as transparent in the community. Clergy wrestle with changing roles and expectations.

When religious see their problems with Church structures as concerns shared with others, they are effective in responding to them. They can critique the Church but also collaborate, dialogue, and live with some of the imperfections that all people in the Church must bear. When they can do this, they are in a better position to give support and receive support from other members of the Church community.

The call of all Christians to holiness, however, is lived out in distinct vocations. All vocations have a manner of living which is socially recognized and publically understood.[6] Religious need to reinterpret the meaning of their vows, with the same seriousness accorded the other vocations, as a choice which limits other choices. Defining the boundaries and the opportunities of religious life enables the next generation to better understand the vowed life and choose it.

A fifth development which effects the theology of the vows is *a new understanding of the person*. In the past, we defined the person through the philosophical understandings of the Middle Ages. A human person was someone with intelligence and free will. This approach was helpful in specifying enduring qualities of human life, but it said little about the meaning of life or its infinite variety. For instance, how much would " a rational animal" describe a close friend?

Today, understandings of the person emphasize human individuality. New theology stresses that people are unique and their actions are specific, individual, and meaningful within a certain time and place. This understanding of both the person and human motivation allows for a more pluralistic understanding of the vows. While the vows retain a core of meaning, a new understanding of the person affirms that religious express their vowed commitment differently according to maturation and life-cycle issues. New theology also upholds the idea that people express their faith accord-

6. James P. Hannigan, *Homosexuality: The Test Case For Christian Sexual Ethics*, 106 n. 6.

ing to their culture. Congregations are more aware today that cultures differ in their expression of the vows and no one culture has a theology of the vows which exhausts their meaning.

If we consider the human personality with a new superficiality, another set of problems can arise. For example, religious can excuse their behavior in community because of their personality profile. Communities can limit their formation program to therapeutic explanations of self-understanding, giving weak theological grounding to their members. Instead of ignoring individuality—a former stumbling block—these behaviors uphold individuality to an extreme. Such an approach erodes an awareness of the common qualities and needs that all persons share and subsequently weakens the basis for community life.

In a sixth development, the vows are seen today not just as a means of holiness for the individual, but also as a *contribution to the Church and the world*. The vows call a person to serve the world and contribute to the renewal of the Church. There is probably no other element which is more key to the reinterpretation of the vows than their relationship to the transformation of the Church and society. Religious commitment is indelibly intertwined with these relationships and will be explored in more detail in the following chapters.

Summary

None of these developments is sufficient for rethinking the foundation of the vows; however, they illustrate foundational shifts in theology which affect their reinterpretation. We will see that the vows are a praxis,[7] a stance from which a religious acts which in turn leads to a new understanding of his or her relationship to God, others, and the world. In this reflection-action-reflection model of life, one knows Jesus through following him in a world which, like his own, stands in need of healing and liberation.

7. For a good description of praxis in the following of Jesus, see: Jon Sobrino, *Christology at the Crossroads*, trans. by John Drury (New York: Orbis Books, 1978).

CHAPTER EIGHT

Testing the Ground of Our Roots

While religious congregations have turned to the world in the last twenty-five years, they have not thoroughly examined the questions of theology which influence their actions. Existentialist, liberation, feminist, and creation theologies are among some of the theologies which have offered religious tools for self-understanding. Congregations have used these theologies well to expand their theological self-understanding and to find religious support for new ministerial action.

Even though religious have found various theological movements to be a corrective lens for renewal, these newer theologies are criticisms of mainstream theology, not total theologies. Each provides a partial view of the Christian life and does not attempt to treat all aspects of the Christian mystery. For instance, liberation theology emphasizes Church-world relationships, but has less to say about sacraments. While theology has broadened vision among religious, a theological pluralism has resulted also. There has not been the time nor the political will to integrate these new theological understandings into a total theology of religious life.

The creation of one congregational theology does not answer this problem. Nevertheless, religious do need to examine the theological issues which influence their decisions. While a uniform theology is not necessary, a shared vision of the Christian life is crucial at this time of renewal.

Members in a congregation can act toward a common goal for different reasons. However, a group cannot set effective goals when understandings of relationships between God, self, others, and the world are contradictory. Conversations about theological viewpoints should enter into decision-making so that a greater understanding can be built regarding how the beliefs of members bear on congregational direction and their understanding of the vows.

There is a growing gap, however, between the experience of religious and the words and symbols used to express the vows. Exposure to different life styles, ideologies, and systems of values, has led religious to think differently about the world and themselves and, consequently, the vows. When the vows remain linked to a world view which no longer reflects the experience of religious, some can feel that the vows no longer have validity.

Another solution to this dilemma is to recognize that the symbols of the vows have to be transformed to be understood today. Central to modern experience is a consciousness of personal autonomy and a sense of responsibility for the world. This means that vows have to be seen as oriented to human development and involved with the construction of a meaningful life, not only for the individual but for the community and society as well.

The examination of deeper theological issues which ground religious life is necessary for this reinterpretation. While this task requires the reflection of many people, I would like to pose three areas of theology which do effect the vows: our understanding of God, the human person, and the world.

God

Some people, today, ask whether religious life has a purpose in today's world. Now that religious congregations have given up many institutional commitments, what meaning does religious life have for the Church and the society? The answer to this question is related to the meaning we think God has for our rapidly changing world.

Men and women understand God differently today because they experience life differently. Their vision of God, in turn, affects the understanding of vows. We will not discuss here whether God is male or female. But the presence of this discussion all around us is an indication that we seek to understand God in a changed culture.[1] Experience and theology are cyclical in understanding the vows. Changes in life-experience affect perceptions of God. In turn, perceptions of God influence understanding of religious life. Let me give a few examples.

Before people had greater control over nature through science, they sought from God an answer to the unexplainable in nature.[2] God was the prime mover who initiated all life. Through observing the movement from cause to effect in the world, people sought to know God. For the person of today, who experiences the power to change in the world, this posture of passivity is not a primary avenue to God. God is found more readily in the experience of initiative and creative action.

In medieval theology, we spoke of God as a perfect act. God brought all potentiality to fulfillment. There was nothing left to be developed in God. The effect of this theology on the Christian life and the vows was evident for centuries. People spoke of their moral effort as that of making perfect actions. They acted in imitation of a God who was a perfect act. The notion of a perfect act of contrition and acting with perfect charity flowed from this theology. Generally, religious no longer think of God in these scholastic terms. God is rarely thought of as immutable, unchangeable, and infinite. They prefer a biblical image of God. God is one who became human, suffered, died, and lives—not apart from them, but in deep relationship to them.

People today no longer seek from God an answer to the unexplainable in nature as their medieval brothers and sisters in faith did. However, they do look to God for an answer to mystery in

1. For some recent studies on feminist images of God, see: Anne Carr, *Transforming Grace: Christian Tradition and Women's Experience* (San Francisco: Harper & Row, 1988); Sandra Schneiders, *Woman and the Word: The Gender of God in the New Testament and the Spirituality of Women* (New York: Paulist Press, 1986); Sallie McFague, *Models of God: Theology for an Ecological, Nuclear Age* (Philadelphia: Fortress, 1987).

2. The following is reflective of contemporary discussions on the experience of God. See, for example: Juan Luis Segundo, *Our Idea of God*, trans. by John Drury (New York: Orbis Books, 1973); *A World of Grace: An Introduction to the Themes and Foundations of Karl Rahner's Theology*, ed. by Leo J. O'Donovan (New York: Seabury Press, 1980).

their lives. The modern experience of mystery gives rise to a different question, however. Does life have any meaning?

People question the meaning of life and the universe. God is no longer the answer to the "how" of natural processes, but God is the answer to the meaning of life. It is not the case that human beings no longer need God since they have advanced in technology. The issue is *how* they need God.

God still orders the world, even in a technological age, by giving it meaning. However, the contemporary person questions the existence of God differently from the way that believers did in previous centuries. This shift in approach to God's existence both challenges and grounds the meaning of religious life today.

For the contemporary person, it would be incomprehensible that there is no God because of the consequences of God's absence. Without God, any hope of victory over death, despair, and hopelessness in life would be impossible. Human limitation would imprison all of human life.

Without God, people who create meaning, order, and direction in this world would be destined to experience constant destruction. Denial of God's existence means human investment has no divine partner and acts only with the power of human limits. The question "Is love worth the effort?" could never be answered with assurance. Human efforts to transform the world through love would fall systematically exhausted in the same measure in which they reached out to transform reality.

Religious congregations, as their primary purpose, witness to the meaning that God's existence brings to life. This is the ground of religious life. However, to be understood, this witness has to touch the life issues which cause people to lose a sense of life's meaning. This is the challenge of our age to religious life.

Today, an atmosphere of nihilism, determinism, and materialism crushes religious belief. Each attitude is institutionalized in contemporary culture, offering an explanation of life divorced from God. Religious congregations can challenge these negative voices— "there is no meaning, we have no options, and, the only value in life is material possessions"—by the quality of their witness.

Can the chastity of religious, through nonpossessive bonding, state that love is worth the effort to a world that fears nothing is meaningful? Can their obedience witness that living within the perimeters of a larger community can free one to love? Can meaningful poverty witness there is more to life than material accumulation? Can its renunciation be transformed into political action for the liberation of others from forced poverty? A shift in our understanding of God should affect our interpretation of the vows because religious speak of the God who exists for them when they live their vows. God's meaning and their meaning are indelibly intertwined.

The human person

Another shift in theology which affects our understanding of the vows centers on the human person. We have stressed that the person is one who gives direction to his or her life and to the world. Theology today describes the freedom to be human as a "freedom from" and a "freedom to." This insight marks a new basis upon which an understanding of the vows can be built.

"Freedom from" is the power within persons to have a certain freedom over themselves and dominion over their world. People take initiative in spite of conditioning forces in their lives. They learn they have the capacity, even though limited by many constraints, to step outside these constraints and make choices.

However, freedom for freedom's sake alone is not enough. Our lives must have direction and purpose. Human freedom involves another capacity, "freedom to." When we form a value system, seek meaning, devise a life plan and act in love, we express our freedom as "freedom to." This more positive part of freedom is not something that develops once we overcome the negative forces in the struggle of "freedom from." Rather, as the creative dimension of freedom, it develops alongside our efforts at self-discipline, and gives a sense of purpose.

Religious life in the past focused heavily on the struggles of "freedom from." The vows helped a person gain mastery over natural instincts and live on a supernatural level. The limitations which were to be overcome, however, were primarily internal. Renunciation was emphasized. We gave up marriage, money, and control over personal decisions in order to devote our lives to God.

A certain view of "freedom from," and subsequently a concept of the person, played a key part in the interpretation of the vows. We emphasized how specific acts, whether it was punctuality, courtesy, or thoroughness, helped to overcome a contrary tendency within us and fulfilled the vows. Fidelity was marked by licit rather than illicit actions, both of which could be clearly defined. In religious life, as well as in Christian morality, appropriate actions were marked by their capacity to express the positive goals of the human personality, in contrast to its negative dimensions. For example, acts of obedience helped to direct the will away from selfishness to its goal of union with the will of God. Even the smallest action could be interpreted within this framework.

Religious life today draws heavily on the concept of "freedom to." We emphasize how our actions express in practical ways the inner orientation of our hearts. Religious have less confidence now that precise behavior can define the meaning of the vows. Fidelity involves responsible relationships rather than fulfillment of rules alone. A wholistic living of the vows means that we take into consideration the intentions which motivate an action and circumstances in which we live in deciding appropriate behavior. Responsibility still develops from the school of love found in the Law. However, fidelity often goes beyond this Law to respond to a broader call to live in relationship to God, others, self, and world in new ways.

The concerns of "freedom from" are still very necessary to a contemporary understanding of the vows; however, self-discipline is "for something" or oriented toward "freedom to." The vows call one to more than a personal perfection unrelated to the world and the development of community. Rather, the vows open a way for responsible adulthood in one's congregation, Church, and society.

Attention to these shifts in theology can help us rearticulate how the vows of poverty, chastity, and obedience uphold a religious experience which always has a place in the faith community. In cherishing religious life, the Church community validates that a call to respond to God can be so deep that fundamental structures of sexual expression, relationship to material things, and decision-making powers will be redirected. However, living in our world today stimulates a new religious experience and expression of these fundamental attitudes. In this chapter, we have outlined some of the new theological issues which face us in re-expressing the vows today.

CHAPTER NINE

The Shifting Ground of World Consciousness

There is a growing sense of world-consciousness today. Even the business world encourages people to have a world-class outlook. The average man or woman's attitude toward the world, however, has changed in more ways than becoming a global consumer. A dramatic shift in the manner in which people view the world influences everyday life. This fresh understanding of the world stems from a variety of sources: a changed experience of the world, a new spirituality, and a different relationship to creation. We will ask in this chapter how these changes influence the way the vows are understood.

In the Middle Ages, people understood the world as fixed. Everything in life was controlled by the laws of nature. It was important to conform to the order of the world and adapt to the rules of society. Since there was little social mobility, a serf did not aspire to be a noble nor did people think about transforming social relationships. This world view had its own soteriological or salvific horizon. The world did not change, and God's will was expressed through an unchanging plan at the heart of reality. Consequently, one was faithful to God by seeking to know this plan and following it.

Today we experience change as normal and look at fidelity very differently. It is unusual for a person to hold the same job for a lifetime or for an entire family to live in the same locality for years. Life is full of new problems without answers. Previous generations did not use life-support systems or question the morality of organ transplants. They did not face the fact that hunger in Africa will leave generations mentally retarded, or that nuclear destruction could end human life. Fidelity to God's will involves more than attention to a fixed plan today; it means seeking answers to new questions.

We see that since the Enlightenment, experience of the world has shifted from a world which was static to one which changes. However, within religious orders, a world of stability remained until the Vatican Council. Even though many congregations participated in the evangelization of the New World and shared its hardships, they did not share its spirit. Religious life existed in a Church which was afraid of modernity.[1] Congregations were bound by a canonical structure which emphasized a monastic approach to community life. Religious congregations maintained the static atmosphere of medieval society even though the world changed around them.

Today, however, religious share many of the same vicissitudes of change that others face in the society: unemployment, unstable family structures, great mobility, concern over finances, and stress. Change, in the experience of the world, influences how religious experience the impact of the vows in daily living. While the values which the vows uphold remain unchanged, their meaning in the lives of religious is marked by a new, world context. For example, religious life no longer offers the security it once promised, nor are religious the people who have answers to life's problems, as authority figures would be in a static world. In fact, just the opposite is the case.

Insecurity is part of the context of living the vows at this time. A great deal of pressure in religious ministry stems from being expected to have answers in many fields. Some religious need to have a working knowledge of general finance, group-process skills, domestic and international political issues, and developments in theology and psychology, to do their ministry. In the midst of these multiple expectations, they have to live with the fact that most issues are open to question. This state of ministry can make religious life and priesthood a rather frightening prospect. In contrast to former vocational expectations of status and security, religious life, at the present, can have challenges which seem impossible to meet.

1. Roger Aubert, "Modernism" in *Encyclopedia of Theology*, ed. by Karl Rahner (New York: Seabury Press, 1975) 969–974.

To live the vows today is to commit oneself to adapt to new circumstances and to be willing to learn in a state of life which is in transition itself. Religious enter into a baptism of loss of authority in order to have adult-to-adult relationships in the Church. They are not always in charge, nor does a religious commitment give them status. Since the vows are not regarded as meaningful in some circles, religious are challenged to communicate with people who have very different understandings of life, without losing a sense of identity. All of these changes free religious, as codisciples with others, for a new understanding of the vows and a new sense of the meaning of their vocation, not based on the world of the past but on a sense of caring and adult responsibility in the world today.

Instead of a higher life that sets them apart, the commitment of the vows brings a religious to the hurts of a changing society. The choice of the vows still calls religious apart, but in a new way. In the face of social change, they cannot choose what some in first-world societies choose. They cannot withdraw into a comfortable haven of individual fulfillment and remain credible. Rather, religious must step into the waters of local and global Church, and through this baptism uncover the prophetic nature of their vows in the world.[2]

Spirituality of the world

A changed world is also reflected in a changed spirituality of the world. In the past, Christians saw the world as a place from which to flee. Religious spoke of going in and out of the world, as if society could be turned off and on like a water faucet. There is no escape from the world today, either in the Christian life *or* religious life. Novices are no longer prepared in a formation foreign to their culture and then sent out into the world. Rather, interaction with society is a constant factor in any process of formation. Work, personal life, and community life are worked out, through, and in relationship to the multiple pressures of a very concrete world.

2. William McConville, "Local Theologies in a World Church: Aloysius Pieris and the Epiphany of Asian Christianity," *New Theology Review*, Vol. 1, No. 3 (August, 1988) 82.

The critical consciousness of the vowed life, symbolized by withdrawal from the world, is understood differently today. In former times, the withdrawal of religious expressed that a religious vocation came from a transcendent source, giving religious a new perspective on the whole of life. Today, religious struggle to express this relationship to God—or a sense of the transcendent—within the world.

Congregations can only witness today to their religious basis in a secular world. Individual religious, in a secularized culture, grapple with the fine line between being part of society yet in a critical posture toward it. Congregations question their public impact. Communities have to express their critical consciousness in concrete ways to communicate their religious basis in a secular world. Religious must be able to point to something in their personal and congregational life that is not simply a religious legitimation of the values of the society in which they live.[3]

The vows today involve ordering priorities for living in society. As a path by which religious enter into society, not withdraw from it, the vows are more a "way of proceeding" than a "means of perfection." While few religious would express their experience of the vows in statements such as, "Now I will practice poverty," or "Now I will call on my vow of chastity," the vows do give direction to choices. Frequently, religious discover the nature of the vows as they encounter ordinary social relationships and decisions. The vows are mystery, but they also have a materiality. They shape, consciously or unconsciously, the categorical or concrete choices a religious makes, compared to others who have different life stances.[4]

3. James E. Cone, *Speaking the Truth: Ecumenism, Liberation and Black Theology* (Grand Rapids, Mich: William B. Eerdmans, 1986) 118.

4. Elizabeth Johnson explains the dynamic implied here in her discussion of the consciousness of Jesus in *Consider Jesus, op. cit.*, 39ff. She draws on the theology of Karl Rahner to discuss how human beings know themselves. All people have an intuitive sense of who they are. This is not a clear notion, rather a general unconscious or pre-thematic self-awareness. However, through action and experience, one comes to a more specific self-knowledge. Different experiences in life help one to self-knowledge in this more precise way. The life of the vows, in this understanding, is a framework which helps in this process. The vows are a categorical choice, a choice which eliminates

As all categorical choices, the vows limit and focus our lives. They exclude certain options which are legitimate for others, and influence decisions which for others would be unnecessary. Fidelity to the vows leads the religious, in a process of self-discovery and conversion, through a distinct way of being Christian. When the vows do not limit or focus choice, because religious have not integrated them with their experience in society, then the relevancy of the vows is questioned. Functionally, the vows can appear to no longer exist.

Religious have difficulty defining the uniqueness of their form of adult Christianity today. However, it is important to remember that choices about how one will express love, share goods, and make decisions continue to set the religious apart.[5] Love, whether it is the love of friendship, marriage, or love of God, which has substance, also has a negative dimension. That is, in order for the content of a life stance to be understood, what is inconsistent with it has to be known.[6] While religious are aware that many things once thought inconsistent with the vows are really legitimate, they still are challenged to name what remains inconsistent with the vowed life today.

Religious often experience the meaning of the vows through wrestling with this challenge of authenticity and consistency. Why don't I sleep with this person whom I love? Why can't I decide this matter without consulting my community? Why won't I take this more prestigious position and leave this Church community to fend for itself? Why must I stretch to move beyond the comfortable boundaries of my friends to bring in the concerns of the global world?

other choices. Through the daily choices which they inspire, they help to translate a general and intuitive sense of self into a more concrete one. By this process, a vocation is grasped at both levels of self-understanding and a "fit" is experienced between a vocational framework and the inner self being developed through the choices implied in that framework.

5. For development of a religious vocation as a categorical or limiting choice in terms of celibacy, see: Mary Anne Huddleston, I.H.M., ed., *Celibate Love: Encounter in Three Dimensions* (New York: Paulist Press, 1984).

6. For a criticism of a vision of love that has no negative boundaries, see: Richard A. McCormick, *Notes on Moral Theology 1965–1980* (Lanham, Md: University Press of America, 1981) 76ff.

In contrast to the days when every detail of the vowed life was expressed in behavioral norms, the vows today are a praxis. They are a way of perceiving, acting, and making decisions. Not just knowing about the vows, but living the vows, unfolds their content to the religious. As a way, the vows are revelation in the deepest biblical sense.[7] When religious shape personal decisions to be consistent with their vows, the deepest part of their lives is revealed—their commitment to God. The vows *do* have a content. When their limits are crossed, the meaning or the mystery which they hide can no longer be found.[8]

The paradox of the vows is that they are understood in an ongoing way, as through a rear-view mirror, when one's baptismal commitment colors decision-making in the midst of the world. The decisions made by a religious are similar to those of all Christians. However, religious experience the call specific to their vocation in daily decisions while sharing in a common struggle of discipleship with all.[9] The Church's support of the vowed life helps religious to own their unique call. It states, "what you experience in the depths of your heart is real. It is a path which others have walked and one which will bring you to life." Vows are made publically to support a religious to live authentically in a world which usually acts contrary to their spirit. A changed spirituality of the vows views this world as the place where religious hear the word of their deepest

7. Margaret Farley, "Fragments for an Ethic of Commitment in Thomas Aquinas," *Journal of Religion*, Vol. 58 (1978) Supplement, *Celebrating the Medieval Heritage: A Colloquy on the thought of Aquinas and Bonaventure*, ed. by David Tracy, 135–155.

8. For another example of a way of life as that which brings insight into the meaning of life, see: Aloysius Pieris, S.J., *Love Meets Wisdom* (New York: Paulist Press, 1988).

9. Richard A. McCormick, "Does Religious Faith Add to Ethical Perception?" in *Readings in Moral Theology, No. 2: The Distinctiveness of Christian Ethics*. Ed. by Charles E. Curran and Richard A. McCormick. (New York: Paulist Press, 1980) 158. It seems this experience of the religious would be analogous to McCormick's description of an existential ethical demand, that is a demand which is not experienced by everyone, rather it comes to an individual at a particular time in history. Here, the relationship of faith to ethical decision-making is discussed under the three transformative experiences. Faith transforms (1) the view of the human person, (2) the motivation in the following of Christ, (3) a style of performing a moral task.

identity and share that word with others. A new spirituality of the world challenges religious congregations also. Charity, characteristic of authentic religious community, has to be transformed into a social charity which makes a statement to the world. Each congregation has to find the societal stances of love which make "see how they love one another" not only a characteristic of the internal life of the community, but representative of its public image before believers and nonbelievers.

As congregations translate their charism in manners which relate to the life issues which touch people in their world, they speak to the deepest hurts of society. This type of response not only expresses the vows through the new spirituality of the world in which the whole Church stands, but also continues to enflesh a congregational charism in terms of the specific world in which it is rooted.

Relationship to creation

A third change in attitude toward the world is a new manner of relating to nature. In the medieval world, nature was seen as a fixed reality. People understood nature through observing cause and effect in created things. Good or bad, or knowledge of God's will, could be known through the laws of nature. For example, in the sexual realm, people observed that children were conceived from sexual intercourse. It was concluded that sexual intercourse was moral only when a couple intended to conceive a child.

People today do not believe that knowledge about what is good or bad is available that clearly through the observation of natural processes alone. Nature provides some information, but not all the information which is needed to make a decision. People today also experience that they can change nature through scientific or medical intervention. Because of this possibility, moral obligation transcends only following the laws of nature. Responsibility for the new nature which we create through scientific advancement weighs heavily on consciences. This same sense of responsibility challenges religious today as a concern about their contribution to ethical guidelines for the next millennium. This search to create a more ethical world is an aspect of their experience of the vows.

The primary goal of religious life is not the development of an ecological ethic or solutions to nuclear warfare. However, a life of poverty, chastity, and obedience makes a statement about the values which should guide the human community in resolving these issues. The contribution which the witness of the vows makes to these ethical questions is through the values which this witness upholds.

Religious congregations, through their ministerial action, also witness to a new moral call in a world in transition. Past generations emphasized the moral dictum, "do good and avoid evil." Today, evil in the world cannot only be avoided; it needs to be transformed. Previously, the Christian life charged us to do the right action in the midst of temptation. Today, the challenge is to also develop the belief within the human community that people are free at all before the megaforces which influence their lives.

In the context of the modern world, religious congregations contribute to a moral atmosphere in which people can believe that they have alternatives to the ways things are. The world no longer suffers from lack of scientific knowledge that bred superstition in the Middle Ages. Today, it suffers from a moral paralysis before the human issues raised by its own technological advances.

These concerns touch the very meaning of religious life because the salvation which Jesus Christ brought is meant to touch anything which alienates human beings. In spite of its affluence, however, the world community faces a mounting ecological crisis and devastating world poverty. Forces which maintain whole countries in servitude and generations in destitution name sin in a new way in our lifetime. Powers which render human life a commodity, from its generation to its termination, negate the truth that "for us and for our salvation, Jesus became human." Religious question by their lives and their ministries the choices which shape the future of the people of our globe. The vows receive a new significance in this historical period through the values they bring to these questions.

Religious congregations can escape the responsibility to face this world in transition by busying themselves with good but irrelevant tasks. To create structures where truly human values can find expression requires that religious creatively participate in movements which ask timely questions and explore new answers. The vows witness, in a world in transition, that the human community lives for more than the present moment. Choices must be made which serve the long-term interests of our globe, not the immediate profit of a few. A challenge for religious congregations is to search out how their own radical dependence on God calls them to collaborative efforts to build a moral atmosphere in the human community. The new world in which religious life is inserted, as in the past, stands in need of its response.

CHAPTER TEN

A Road to Heaven or the New Earth?

There are two trends in the interpretation of the vows today. One emphasizes the call to holiness in religious life and the other stresses the importance of ministry and social transformation. These emphases produce different interpretations of the meaning of the vows. The tension between the two is one between a "heavenly" and a "new earth" view of the vows. Usually, when such polarities are drawn, they produce a false picture of the vows. Religious with a wholistic view of their lives know both views are necessary. However, most religious have not integrated both views into their lives and struggle today to synthesize the two.

One tension in achieving this synthesis centers around language. Religious use spiritual language to describe the reflective rather than the active dimensions of their lives. Theological and spiritual words refer to holiness as passivity and listening. Just as pointedly, religious talk about action and mission with socio-political language: they build the Kingdom and enter into transforming action. The problem is that neither language can fully express the vows today. When religious life is described in terms of ministry or justice, people can feel uneasy that the deep religious experience which lies at its heart is not addressed. When it is discussed in terms of holiness, its relevancy to human suffering is questioned.

The challenge before congregations today is to develop a vision and language about religious life which integrates the two perspectives. Stress on passivity and listening is too "heavenly" for modern people, who expect to make a contribution to the world. Emphasis on building the "new earth" can be careerism if it isn't linked to the religious experience which grounds religious commitment. Some of the foundations of a new synthesis and their practical ramifications are discussed in the following chapters. For now, we will explore the values upheld by a "heavenly" and a "new earth" view of the vows.

A heavenly view of the vows

A "heavenly" view of the vows is built upon certain theological beliefs. These beliefs are not found explicitly in the theology of the vows; however, they reflect a spirituality which upholds them. A "heavenly" approach stresses that the Incarnation and Redemption of Jesus Christ brought a new era to human history, the fullness of time.[1] This spirituality focuses on the ultimate meaning of life. Human life is meant to bring men and women face-to-face with God in God's Kingdom, power, and glory. Human existence is judged in each moment by the Word of God. Religious commitment, consequently, is a response to the ultimate meaning of life. It is a total gift of self to God. To make vows is to unite oneself to the redemptive love of Jesus Christ for all of one's life.

The practice of the vows before the council reflected this theology and spirituality. Religious focused on the ultimate values which lay at the heart of their commitment. Meditations on death, the rule of silence, the underplaying of personal ministry, the anonymity of relationships, were supported by this spirituality. Human life was passing and the real meaning of life was found in its significance for heaven.

A "heavenly" view of the vows stresses that religious life belongs integrally to the life of the Church and witnesses to the mystery of its life. Religious recognize that the culminating, decisive happening of history has already taken place with the coming of Jesus Christ. Vows are a response to this.

The "heavenly" view of the vows should not be associated only with a pre-Vatican view of religious life. It contains perennial values essential for today. God's definitive judgment has begun. The entire order of the world and human life is a summons and judgment

1. For a discussion of the contrast between these two views, see: Juan Luis Segundo, *The Liberation of Theology*, trans. by John Drury (New York: Orbis Books, 1976) 122ff.

of God. No matter what degree of human progress is accomplished, human life will never be otherwise. The final action of God will always be needed to restore the justice that history has not produced in its visible events.

All of these theological insights have a place in the religious life of the future. They ground religious vows as an act of radical openness to God's action as the most definitive aspect of life. They emphasize the counsels of the gospel as the central vision of religious commitment.

One present difficulty with integrating these insights into a theology of the vows is that most religious live in a secular atmosphere. The spirituality which supports a "heavenly" focus is not as meaningful today as it was in the past. The structure of pre-Vatican religious life, since it was removed from ordinary society, held these ultimate truths before the religious daily. Religious who live in a secular world do not have these supports. Religious today need new ways to connect with their otherworldly focus while also addressing the concern of the modern person: how to contribute to this world. For this to occur, a "heavenly" view of the vows has to be integrated with another, more this-worldly religious perspective.

Seeing life from another perspective

A "new earth" view of the vows also has a theological foundation. Instead of emphasizing that Jesus Christ has already brought salvation through his Incarnation and Redemption, it stresses that the full effect of salvation is still to be brought to completion in human history.[2] Human life is in the process of becoming the Reign of God. The Church is the sign, instrument, and herald of this ongoing reality.

It is no surprise that a "new earth" perspective approaches religious life differently. Instead of asking the significance of the vows for heaven, a "new earth" perspective questions their meaning for this life. The vows are considered for their relevance in helping people become more fully human and shaping the human community. Persons with a "new earth" perspective ask what will hap-

2. This theme is developed in terms of our understanding of Jesus in Elizabeth Johnson, *Consider Jesus, op. cit.*, chapters 1–4.

pen in their lives and in this world because they have chosen a vowed life.

People today ask this question about religious commitment, which does not mean they are unconcerned about the next life, or lack a religious perspective, or feel they do not need God. Their question simply indicates that God's importance in their lives is expressed in a pragmatic manner.

Modern persons are empirical, practical, and oriented toward making things better. Hence, they express God's importance in their lives by asking what God's place is in their decision-making. They question how belief in God affects their priorities: What is important to God in this life? Before God's eyes what will last? What is worth our efforts? What do we want our lives to stand for? Is this what God stands for?

For people who are autonomous and have many adult options, religious life has to answer the above questions. More underlies these questions than a pragmaticism about successful work or results. People need to know that religious life is a way to express a deep religious experience in action and to continue to discover, through creative action, a personal relationship with God. For religious life to be meaningful, this ongoing experience of both radical action and radical discovery is needed.

It is at this point that the limitations of a "heavenly" view of the vows appear. Why is this so? The beliefs of the "heavenly" perspective affirm what is ultimately important. The belief that we stand before God helps us to discern right from wrong. The fact of eternity points to the deeper meaning of human life in these complex times. But this is not enough.

Today, religious need to know how the beliefs about the next world make an impact on choices in the present.[3] Why do religious give their lives in Central America? Why does a successful computer analyst leave a top-ten company and use his skill in a religious congregation? Why would a financially secure woman give up her condo and join others in a hospital ministry? Why do two people in love choose not to express that love genitally because of their primary

3. See *Gaudium et Spes* 21. "A hope related to the end of time does not diminish the importance of intervening duties, but rather undergirds the acquittal of them with fresh incentives." *The Documents of Vatican II,* ed. by Walter M. Abbott (New York: Herder and Herder, 1966).

commitment? Why tackle the justice or ecclesial questions of our day? Why not settle into a comfortable niche and allow the world to go by?

While a "heavenly" view of the vows emphasizes the importance of a person's relationship with God, a "new earth" perspective probes the ramfications of this relationship in the here and now. Religious have to know Jesus Christ as a person, not just for the hereafter, but for the present, in order for their lives to have meaning.[4] The happiness of religious depends on their interpreting Jesus' message and following it.[5] The "new earth" approach does not emphasize Jesus' ultimate significance but his attitudes, his style of life, his interests, and his values. Religious ponder the life of Jesus to see how he lived out the values of the Reign of God so that they can do the same when institutional crises, ministry burn-out, health needs, gender issues, and living among skeptics challenge them everyday.

Religious look to Jesus for more than a model or example. As they confront issues not faced by Jesus in the first century, they develop a relationship with Jesus which transforms their own lives and that of the world. The vows state that the personal fulfillment of a religious in this life is centered ultimately in this mystery. As an adult stance in the Church a vowed commitment leads one to heaven, but it also leads one to a fulfilled life focused on values which bring about God's reign on earth.

While each vocation in the Church witnesses to the importance of relationship with God, religious witness to this relationship by making it the total focus of their lives. Their choice affirms God's interest in all of life. The pursuit of healthy relationships, economic realities, health, peace, and wholeness that occupies the major part of human energies are also God's interest. Religious express their hope in God through their own reliance on God in life. In face of the meaninglessness and determinism which characterize modern culture, religious affirm that human life, even when oppressed, will be made new by God's own power.

Modern-day religious witness to a God working now in history in a different way from the monk of the fourth century or the

4. Juan Luis Segundo, *Our Idea of God, op. cit.,* 93.
5. *Gaudium et Spes,* 44.

cloistered nun of Renaissance Europe. However, the common denominator among generations of religious is the inevitable question which flows from the call to love—the meaning of suffering and the cross.[6]

The love expressed through the vows is a sign that all love and its resulting suffering has ultimate significance. This is the eschatological witness of religious life. However, it is only if this love meets the suffering of this world that religious life is a life stance worth the effort in our times. This is what the "new earth" perspective upholds. Each generation of religious must take its turn asking these questions of the paschal mystery: Is death for resurrection? Is love worth the effort? Does it pay to be countercultural?

The "new earth" view of the vows affirms that eschatology is not just a fact about the next world, but that God's power is related to today. God's action is not only the last thing in each human life; it is also central to living in the present. Hence, the Reign or Kingdom of God is not only the goal of human life but its ongoing project.

The "new earth" perspective challenges religious congregations to make the ultimate reality of God's final action not just information about the next world, but the project of this one. We will explore this vision for religious congregations, examining the ramifications of the "new earth" perspective for corporate life. We will look at the vows as a project, as a social reality, and as a concrete sign of God in the world.

6. Juan Luis Segundo, *The Sacraments Today*, trans. by John Drury (New York: Orbis Books, 1973) 56.

CHAPTER ELEVEN

Vows for an Earthly Journey

The Kingdom of God points to the relationship between God and human beings.[1] In God's Kingdom, first place is given to those who suffer. In a "new earth" perspective, building relationships characteristic of the Reign of God is part of religious life. As do all who are baptized, religious enter into a lifelong pursuit of the concerns of the Kingdom which they make their own.

Even though God creates the Kingdom, human beings have an important role in bringing it about. In this way, the Kingdom is a project. However, the Kingdom is not just something we bring about; it also happens to us and calls us. The Reign of God breaks through in history, bringing love and liberation to individuals and groups. We can examine how religious join their lives to the dynamic of the Kingdom by considering religious life from three perspectives: as a life project of seeking the Kingdom, as a way of life having a social dimension, and as a concrete sign in the world.

The vows and the kingdom: a project of life

A "new earth" perspective emphasizes the role of human initiative in religious life. Religious can and should create conditions where God's Reign can come. The Kingdom is more than a call to perfection; it is the project of religious life itself. Through the vows, religious promise to invest their energy, which could have been invested in personal concerns alone, into the construction of

1. Juan Luis Segundo, *The Liberation of Theology*, 87.

the "new earth." Through this investment, the gospel call to be perfect is fulfilled.

Religious life is a faith stance. Through the vows, religious state that the project of their lives is one which does not have meaning without religious faith. Even though religious share the same baptismal call as all Christians, they possess a unique ability to witness to God's presence as ultimately important in life. While all vocations do this, the symbols of religious life have a different density with which to bear this witness, if they are lived out authentically. Why is this so?

Density is the capacity of a symbol to bear many levels of meaning. The choice of celibacy, poverty, and obedience for a life stance involves a different life project from that which most people undertake. The primary pursuit of family life, personal possessions, and a type of control over goals is laid aside. The vows plunge religious into community, challenging the cultural stance that self-fulfillment is an act of personal accomplishment alone. This commitment to community-building over the long haul stands in contrast to an individualistic mentality. Religious life also is based on a life covenant among people not bound by blood or marriage. In a religious congregation, members from many races and cultures can seek to live multiculturally.

When people observe religious laying aside legitimate life goals and note the values around which they bond, they raise natural questions: Why? What are these persons about in life? Religious life involves more than social action, professional excellence, or holistic living. Rather, it is a life project built on a relationship. The vows witness that a personal God is the silent support of a life of active love. This love is real, the kind that can invest itself to the point of devotion.[2]

Friendship and community life certainly bring God's love home to the life of a religious. However, a celibate life also requires the capacity for solitude. Religious life provides structural support for contemplation that no other vocation provides.[3] The solitude in

2. David Hassel discusses this at length in his book *Searching the Limits of Love: An Approach to the Secular Transcendent God* (Chicago: Loyola University Press, 1985).

3. See: Andre Guindon, *The Sexual Creators* (Lanham, Md: University Press of America, 1986) 205ff.

the life of a religious can bring loneliness at times. However, solitude feeds not only a relationship with God but also an awareness of God's cause, the Kingdom, at the heart of a religious vocation.

To make vows is to state that material things, sexual partnership, and complete freedom of choice are not as important to religious as the fullness of life to which God has called them. We refer to this fullness of life when we pray, "Your Kingdom come." The vows not only give direction to an individual life, they make a statement about the right of all persons to seek fullness of life.

A "new earth" view of the vows emphasizes that the gospel values of celibate chastity, poverty, and obedience center the life project of the religious around the concerns of the Kingdom. Poverty, chastity, and obedience will not be just aspects of their Christian life, as they are for all Christians. Rather, they will be primary life stances that will affect how a religious lives out all the other gospel values in the pursuit of the Kingdom.

The love which inspires a vowed commitment is, in itself, an expression of the Kingdom. Love shared in relationships which serve human need will also endure in the "new earth" when God comes again. As Paul notes, many things will pass away that we think are important. Only love will last, because love already shares in God's final love which brings all things to fulfillment. This is the love which invests now in the project of the Kingdom. It is an affair of the heart in which religious build the Reign of God and in the process meet not only the needs of the world, but also God.[4]

Congregations and the "new earth"

A "new earth" view of the vows challenges congregations to build a common vision so that they can act corporately. By acting corporately, congregations have the ability to build the Kingdom in a manner in which individual Christians cannot. A communal charism sets the direction for Kingdom building and provides a focus for discernment of congregational calls.

The particular charism of a community is a special insight into the nature of the Reign of God. The charism of my own community, for example, is the Goodness of God and an option for the

4. See: Wilkie Au, *By Way of the Heart* (New York: Paulist Press, 1989).

poor. This is one dimension of the Kingdom and the values for which it stands. A charism is not just an inspiration; it has practical implications. By celebrating and living its charism, a congregation not only witnesses to something about God's life, but how things ought to be in human life.

The pursuit of the Kingdom as a project always involves unfinished business. A charism such as mercy, providence, or the goodness of God has to be translated not only into an overall vision but into concrete projects and goals. Through these practical means, a community seeks the Kingdom by closing the gap between what ought to be and what is. However, a community can only live out its charism in a partial manner. For instance, a charism can inspire a ministerial project in a local church. The charism remains partially unexpressed, however, because all projects have limited success, and even successful projects leave unexpressed the fullness of the Kingdom.

However, focusing on the Kingdom as a project can help congregations realize that there are no ''Christian solutions'' to problems today. There is no one answer. There is only the relative value of some courses of action over others. Since there is no perfect solution, communities have to weigh and measure alternatives in seeking the best response to the call of the Kingdom to them as a group.

New values and attitudes are needed in congregations today for this type of participation in the concerns of the Kingdom. One of them is the need for creativity. Religious need creativity in order to create efficacious responses to new problems. The single concern for doing right needs to be blended into an outlook which embraces planning and dreaming. The Spirit works in both.

The vows as a social stance

The vows are meant to affect the world. In the past, we emphasized their power to develop the Reign of God within the religious and lead them to perfection. Today, we stress that the Reign of God exists not only in our hearts but in the world, making an impact on both personal and social life. The Kingdom not only grows in individuals, but in groups, nations, agencies, attitudes, races, and cultures. While formerly we stressed that the vows had a social import through a commitment to a collective or institutional life, today we ask their relevance for a new type of public and corporate life.

The call of the Kingdom within us is important. It prompts us to question whether our actions are love or egoism. The Reign of God calls people away from their idols to a closer following after Jesus. A "new earth" perspective, however, adds another dimension to this reflection. It probes the social relevance of an action. It asks what will last or endure in human life because of this action.

This question can shed new light on old values in religious congregations. The progress of the Kingdom is often slow and complex. Realizing the difficulty with which Kingdom values are realized highlights the value of institutions. Institutions can engage in affirmative action and protest long after the individuals in them have given up their individual roles. Newer members affirm the positive role of institutions in their life choice. They enter religious life so that their individual efforts can be taken up into a collective whole. This sense of being part of something bigger than oneself and finding strength for individual efforts in this realization is an experience of the social reality of the Kingdom at work.

Planning in religious congregations also can be given new value through a "new earth" perspective. While most congregations have drawn upon management techniques for decades, a "new earth" perspective draws out the theological significance of these efforts. Things can only happen from above when they have been prepared "from below." Essential to bringing about the Kingdom today is the ability to draw upon the wisdom of good management techniques in congregational planning.

Impersonal conduct can also be part of the Reign of God. A "heavenly" perspective supports the integrity of personal action. This perspective alone, however, can lead to passivity and individualism in the face of the responsibility to contribute to corporate life or society. Significant social changes are not just the result of free personal decisions. Rather, they proceed from more impersonal factors such as legislation, group action, and constructive power techniques which often obscure the distinctions and awareness of individual differences maintained on a more personal level. These behaviors also can be integrated into the life of the vows.

Confusion over the idea that the Kingdom requires that social change have personal consent can lead to the assumption that the only Christian path to social change is that which results from universal consensus. This, too, can lead to a subtle support of Christian passivity. Religious congregations can find themselves in a position of waiting and hoping, expecting that every individual religious will grasp the meaning of the gospel's demands in the same way and that new life will come from this consensus.

On the contrary, the need for authority in religious life has always challenged this myth. It has asserted that the demands of the mission to bring about the Kingdom mean that the inherent passivity which comes from an overreliance on group consensus has to be balanced by leadership conducted in an adult manner and by the call to common goals.

The vows as a concrete sign in the world

The vows are to be a concrete sign in the world. The Kingdom is meant to be known and experienced in the present, not only to be a motivation for the next life. In a "heavenly" perspective on the vows, God's action is absolute. God is ultimately victorious even if we cannot perceive it immediately. God's providence guides all things. People accept that God's ways are not their ways.

The "new earth" perspective takes another approach. The Church and religious life are not only signs of the eschatological kingdom at the end of time; rather, they are to be effective now. The Church and religious life are called to bring light to the problems of the human condition viewed nightly on the news.

Religious congregations thus have a new imperative. Not only should individual religious be a sign in the world, but the religious community as a whole is a sign.[5] To be this sign, the corporate life of the congregation has to have the faith structure of discipleship in the Kingdom, the paschal mystery. Congregations live the paschal mystery as they take responsibility to address the problems of our times.[6] Their corporate life witnesses to the truth that the capacity to move beyond self to the good of the other is that which creates love in the world.

5. Thomas Clarke, S.J., "Jesuit Commitment—Fraternal Covenant?," *op. cit.*, 82ff.

6. Juan Luis Segundo, *Our Idea of God, op. cit.*, 175.

Hence, to be a sign, religious orders have to be more than a mere juxtaposition of persons who say, think, and do things that are completely different or even opposed to each other.[7] Since vows are made in community, religious are called to more than a private fidelity to the vows; rather, they are called also to the public and communal decisions which the vows inspire. Since the Church is visible in society through its public institutions, religious congregations still have a powerful role in this visibility. As congregations create new institutions, works, and a corporate life, they take up this responsibility for public witness.

In their reinterpretation of religious life, congregations must ask how the vows remain an eschatological sign. To do this, both a "heavenly" and a "new earth" view of the vows are needed. The "heavenly" perspective will guide them in asking what is ultimately important. The "new earth" perspective will ask them to discern the significance of their corporate efforts. What will last? What is worth their effort?

This search is not new. Religious congregations have always been called to give witness to the presence of the Kingdom and its transforming life. Today, congregations remember the promise that what human effort cannot accomplish, God will complete in the final eschatological action. But what human effort has accomplished will not be lost at the end of time. Their histories and their present moment both will be celebrated. Finally, what human effort could have accomplished—and did not—will be judged with the full justice of the eschatological judgment.

Religious congregations are called to integrate the "heavenly" and "new earth" perspectives on the vows, as religious life is asked to speak its truth to new peoples and generations. These new members bring to this task of integration a passion for life and a sense of their capacity for transformative action. As congregations respond, they too become part of the new earth in the making as religious reinterpret their life for the new millennium.

7. Juan Luis Segundo, *The Sacraments Today, op. cit.,* 68.

PART FOUR

Current Issues in Religious Life

CHAPTER TWELVE

Community Life: Finding the Golden Shadow of Individualism

The culture of individualism has issued a death warrant to community life in religious orders. Social scientists claim that people in society find it difficult to even think on a group or a communal level.[1] If their perceptions are accurate, those who predict a future religious life without community may be right. This period of transition, on the other hand, may provide an unparalleled opportunity for community life to be resymbolized in the Church. Whether the future will hold one or the other option is not inevitable; rather, it is a matter of choice and strategy for religious today.

The mixed quality of religious life

Religious life has been both a countercultural and a transformative force in the society. The two do not always go together. When a religious movement is able to be both countercultural and transformative, it has a hybrid or mixed nature to it.[2] To have this mixed quality, a group must be enough unlike the society to stand

1. Robert Bellah in *Habits of the Heart, op. cit.*, claims the American way of thinking is so individualistic that it lacks concepts for things of a communal nature.

2. John Coleman, *An American Strategic Theology*, (New York: Paulist Press, 1982) 38–56.

in contrast to it. Its common life should reflect its transcendent source of inspiration, and it should have the capacity to be critical of the prevailing understanding of things in the culture. On the other hand, a group should be enough like the culture, that the religious and human meaning upon which it is based can be communicated. People only identify with something not foreign to their way of thinking and being. Theologians affirm that God reveals to us according to our ordinary ways of understanding. Groups are understood also within these boundaries.

This mixed quality is not easily achieved in religious congregations. One by-product of seeking to be in the culture, and not of it, is a sense of malaise in religious communities today. This has resulted from movement away from a separated life to a connected life style with families, friends, and society. Living this way has brought new life both to religious and to congregations. The malaise stems from the loneliness, isolation, and collapse of a sense of community that has resulted from struggling to live in new ways with uneven success.

The resolution of the tension is discussed often in community today. Conversations take two directions. Some call for a return to "community," which sends chills down the spines of others as fears of restriction, enclosure, and controlled living well up from their past. Others prophesy an end to community, a final liberation from its myths. They predict it will be replaced by loosely connected networks of adults gathered in support groups while living individually. The first group retorts that this scenario replaces the face-to-face living and commitment of community life with "drinks and dinner when we feel like it." The second group answers that community life is not working for many religious, and new things have to be tried to fill the vacuum.

The individuals involved in these conversations know that the future needs more than the present situation of community life can provide. While there will always be a need for individual living arrangements in religious congregations other than just a group setting, the general living of community life today still calls for a deep resymbolization.

Taken alone, neither of the directions discussed above will be the future of community life. Religious orders cannot return to a medieval collective and be incarnated in the modern world. Individualism is part of the cultural matrix of our society. Nor can they adopt the individualistic lifestyle of the culture and rename it with religious terms, while at the same time effectively offering an alternative lifestyle to the Church. The challenge to congregations today is to learn about community life from individualism, but also to critique its fallacies. If religious can do this, they will not only revitalize their own communities but will also make a contribution to a society which also needs community.

Reclaiming our shadow

As congregations reflect on their lives over the last thirty years, individualism is one shadow of renewal. It is part of the collective fallout that was not listed in the congregational plan. Individualism, or attention to individuals without due regard for group or relational realities, is a negative quality of first-world culture. It is associated with selfishness, relational breakdown, and personal destruction.

Religious experience individualism as a breakdown of community life. People seem to have little commitment to each other. Communities are not a place where people spend time. Patterns of practice such as times of prayer, recreation, reconciliation, and outreach are not experienced collectively. There is an uncertainty that community members can be counted on even in times of crisis such as illness, funerals, and transitions.

To learn from individualism, religious have to find the gold that is hidden in this shadow experience. This approach is referred to in psychological literature today as retrieving one's golden shadow.[3] On a personal level, the process involves looking at a negative aspect of one's personality which has been previously repressed and seeking to find its creative and constructive aspects. The negative characteristic is reappropriated into the self, not in its distorted, repressed form, but through the visualization of an appropriate expression of it in its healing qualities.

This process can also be done collectively. If individual religious and congregations today can look at individualism in their lives, it could provide a rich and healing source for imaging the religious community of the future.

3. William Miller, *Your Golden Shadow, op. cit.*

Reappropriating individualism into community life

Individualism has forced religious to face the damage done to persons when institutional and communal needs are given priority to such an extent that individual talents and differences are ignored. It has alerted groups to the dysfunctional results of "forced feeding" community values to the exclusion of welcoming the dreams of each member. Emphasis on the individual has also brought the lonely discovery of the difference between virtue when supported by group example and that which religious actually do on their own.

Experiments in shared authority on the local level have also been part of an individualistic trend in religious congregations. Shared authority is not as easy as people thought; it requires self sacrifice and communication, and it fails at times to serve human needs. In horizontal communities, also outgrowths of individualistic patterns, many insights have been gained. Life in the institution hid some responsibilities of adult life. Local communities have discovered there is no more love in them than individuals are willing to put into them. Their emptiness at times is not the fault of the central administration, the Pope, or congregational structures, but rather the envy, competitiveness, and refusal to leave enough time in professional schedules to "pencil in" brothers and sisters in community.

Some religious have learned there are no magic godmothers or godfathers to fix things when they go wrong. As individualism has helped many of them to move away from tightly controlled structures, it has also shown them that their own addictions can no longer remain hidden.

Struggle over community life

Community life has been the source of prolonged anger, guilt, and despair for some religious.[4] One cause of this anger is an image of community from a real or imagined past. Religious conclude that, since no one will ever be good enough at community, it is best to give it up. The pragmatic thing to do is to drop the possibility of ever living it. Others point out that the goal was simply foolish

4. This is discussed in David Hassel, *Healing the Ache of Alienation* (New York: Paulist Press, 1990).

in the first place. Group living centered on mission is unrealistic except among intentional friends.

Instead of approaching individualism as a shadow, the above approach sees it as the future. The solution faces the shadow of individualism in religious life, but does not go beyond it. Another possibility is to go beyond individualism by finding, in an apparent death of community, a sense of its hidden life. It is only by confrontation, reordering, and renewal that this shadow can be named and what is golden in it can be retrieved.

Practically, this means what works and does not work in religious community has to be faced. Expectations which serve neither the persons nor the mission have to be dropped. Real needs have to be brought to the surface and new symbols and rituals have to be discovered by groups willing to risk continued experimentation with living together.

Beyond enclaves

Even though new community styles have surfaced during renewal, the bond which holds them together is weak. Some groups formed in flight. Fleeing an over-institutionalized life, religious sought what was denied to them in a larger group. Agreement regarding common recreations, meals together, house maintenance, and hospitality proved to be a welcome relief to constant struggle over these basic areas of daily life.

However, after some years of living together, people raise the question of how their life together as religious differs from that of a group of people who share an apartment and live their separate professional lives. This is not a new question in the Church. St. Augustine once commented that even a band of robbers has community. They have a way to order their lives, split up their revenue, and prosper as a group. Obviously, in religious life, we are looking for something more.

To strengthen the bond of community, community life has to be grounded on a new image. Communities once were taken for granted because they were linked to visible ministries. This is no longer the case. A negative bonding, built on what is being escaped in structured situations, is not enough. The bonding of intentional friendship, while beautiful in itself, lacks the fluidity and inclusiveness of religious community. What is needed today are new symbols and rituals to link symbols of faith to an enlivened sense of community.

New rituals and symbols

Groups have not found ways to reincorporate the common symbols and rituals of faith, which were part of the older institutional structure, into new styles of community living. Instead, faith has been personalized and privatized while community is formed around commonly decided needs. Religious, however, have to know what draws them together beyond their common agreement. Common symbols and rituals of faith constantly bring this to mind.

Symbol and ritual, more than intellectual convictions, motivate people to come together as community. However, today, old rituals do not fit and new rituals have not been created. Rituals institutionalized in religious communities in the past were tied to notions of the extended family. Members no longer think of their relationship in these terms. The superior is no longer seen as the mother or father of a family, leading meal prayers or receiving a renewal of baptismal promises on an anniversary. Rituals in the past also reflected a stratified world which mirrored the hierarchical side of the Church. Places in convent and monastery chapels were ordered according to entrance date. Religious communities no longer function in this way.

As forms of self-understanding were dropped, so were the rituals. However, communities can associate traditions of healing, bonding, forgiving, and sharing of faith with former models. New ways of community living did evolve new types of "rituals," but these lacked a ritualized or repetitive nature. Rather than regular occurrences, experimentation with new forms of prayer and the inclusion of a variety of experiences were more commonplace.

Symbols and rituals are a second story to members which give their personal stories meaning. Through symbols, they answer the question about what difference it makes whether they belong to this group or not. Common beliefs are ritualized in a manner which draws members to the larger meaning which holds them together. Faith rituals help to form the community in such a way that members can identify how their living together is different from that of a group of professionals who share expenses in a living situation.

Individuals may find a sense of comfort in a group because of shared preferences. But after a time, people fail to find meaning in the group. Without shared symbols and rituals, the basis of community life is not transpersonal. The group does not move beyond itself, and life together is not mutually evangelizing. We live in a world where people have several, often conflicting, world views. Without common rituals and symbols of faith, individuals will not be able to find in community life an alternative-meaning system which continually enlivens them.

Why has this not occurred in communities? In some instances, anything repetitive or traditional was considered divorced from the new culture of greater identification with the secular society. In other cases, adoption of new symbols in tune with the culture was so intense that another belief system was institutionalized—some form of secularism.

Religious also created rituals privately according to individual preferences. Others replaced tradition by a pseudo-tradition of how things were, or how they wished to remember them. Rituals and symbols were used for common nostalgia but not for a common vision to support interaction with today's culture.

Symbols were adopted based on what was survived together. The recalling of these stories became the ritual.[5] However, if this is all that occurs in a community, no countersymbols or new experiences can penetrate this atmosphere. This forms an old- (although age may not be a factor) girl or old-boy mentality in a congregation, and the community then becomes an enclave. There is a tacit agreement among its members not to invest energy into creating a common future, but merely to continue as they are. While it may take them a few years to discover this reality, new members will go away sad when they uncover the real consensus upon which the active community is built.

While there are no ready-made symbols, there are some directions which congregations can take to examine together this aspect of their life. First, they can discuss their present communal patterns and identify the common symbols they have already tried to reinstitute. Second, local communities and support groups can reflect together, not on the symbols they "should" use, but on what

5. Mary Jo Leddy, "Beyond the Liberal Model," *op. cit.*, 46.

they truly want to use. Third, congregations, especially women's groups, can reflect on the role of sacramental life in their corporate life. They can address the present alienation felt by some members regarding the sacraments because of the lack of women's ordination. They can seek constructive ways to continue to share in the life of the sacraments and the liturgical prayer of the Church. Both men and women's groups can examine the inclusiveness of their prayer and the gender relationships their public prayer symbolizes.

Finally, new faith symbols and rituals cannot be used in isolation from authentic living. New rituals are not the answer to a renewal of community life. We need to realize today that members of a religious congregation can be committed, yet their witness can fail to engage the next generation. New symbols and rituals must be able to transmit values to the next generation. A key factor in this transmission is a holistic sense of community itself. It is to the characteristics of a sense of community to which we will now turn our attention.

CHAPTER THIRTEEN

Toward a Transformative Community

The religious experience central to Christianity is that of being loved by a personal God. Community life is meant to bear witness to this experience. There is a crisis surrounding community life today, since it is unclear how we are to live communally in a secular world. Modern living militates against communal forms of life. A society which is competitive, individualistic, and mobile makes it difficult to form community.

However, community life retains a place even in this new setting. Religious today are immersed in ministries whose stresses mirror the complexities of today's society. What role does community play in this new ministerial setting? It may be helpful to think of community as one moment in a living cycle where ministry and community occur in an interactive balance.

Insertion into ministry

As in the Church, mission determines the structure of a religious community. Commitment to mission is the first movement of the living cycle of religious life since ministry expresses the love of God and God's people which grounds religious life.

The experience of ministry, however, places religious immediately into structures often inimical to the values of gospel living. Ministry takes place in a clear, hierarchical order of profession, with all of its stresses and compromises. Forces which act against the values of the Kingdom affect every ministerial decision and take their toll of the energies of religious.[1]

Members of religious communities experience the fact that structures can block and promote their initiatives in an unpredictable manner. Organizational systems can turn and twist an initial project until it is unrecognizable. Religious can feel helpless as needs and issues evade their grasp in ministry. Persons and events can appear like objects carried swiftly away by a river current, far beyond the range of ministerial intervention. Entering into ministry creates a need for support, analysis, and vision.

Community life

Community living has the potential to create both a liminality, or a breakdown of boundaries which are experienced in ministry, and an experience of the Absolute who grounds life and love. Community forms the second movement in the living cycle of religious.

In the Acts of the Apostles, early communities are described as sharing "all things in common." It is doubtful that this ideal was fully realized, as we note in the story of Ananias and Saphira. However, this image provides an example of the contrast-experience of community life. [Acts 5:1]. The Christian vision altered daily living and created a contrast-experience which gave hope and direction.

Through community life, religious learn the meaning of their congregation. Through the way community is lived and the values which are upheld in its codes, rituals, and patterns of practice, they discover the gospel vision at the heart of their congregation. The means to grow in those values can be found in community, as the

1. These types of societal repressions are discussed in Herbert Marcuse, *Eros and Civilization* (Boston: Beacon Press, 1966) 37ff., 87ff. See also Reinhold Niebuhr, *Moral Man and Immoral Society* (New York: Charles Scribner's Sons, 1932). For cultural expressions, see: Virgil Elizondo, *Galilean Journey: The Mexican-American Promise* (New York: Orbis, 1985); Allan Boesak, *Walking on Thorns: The Call to Christian Obedience* (Grand Rapids, Mich.: William B. Eerdmanns, 1984); Madonna Kolbenschlag, *Lost in the Land of Oz, op. cit.*; James Cone, *Speaking the Truth, op. cit.*; *Lift Every Voice: Constructing Christian Theologies from the Underside*, ed. by Susan Brooks Thistlewaite and Mary Potter Engels (San Francisco: Harper & Row, 1990).

vision and discipline of gospel living is experienced daily. Community is the visible social model where a congregational way of life can be observed, measured against others, and selected as a way of living. As part of the way religious life brings people to God, community living forms a central aspect of a religious vocation.[2]

Reflection

The living cycle of religious also involves prayerful reflection. Besides the personal prayer of members, a community needs to interpret its congregational texts and the Scriptures in a manner which is relevant to their lives. Hermeneutics is the science of how and by what standards a text is interpreted. When a community corporately reflects on the gospel and its constitutions, it engages in a hermeneutical task.

Scripture and congregational texts can only be interpreted by a living community. This is not a task for individuals alone. It is only by a common religiosity that the relevance of the texts are unlocked in a new situation and in new times. In other words, only authentic living makes it possible to interpret the texts of the community.[3] The source of renewal, in the Church and in religious congregations, is not in philosophies or theological speculation, surveys or formation alone. It springs from the communal religiosity, living authentically a charismatic call in relationship to real needs.

Since living community forms the basis of interpretation of its congregational texts and Scriptures, the quality of community living is important.[4] Prayer, rituals, and patterns of practice, which

2. Aloysius Pieris, *An Asian Theology of Liberation* (New York: Orbis Books, 1988) 53.

3. David Tracy, "Hermeneutical Reflections in the New Paradigm," in *Paradigm Change in Theology*, ed. by Hans Küng and David Tracy (New York: Crossroads, 1989) 34–62.

4. For a reflection on qualities of this religiosity in the future, see: "Transformative Elements in Religious Life," unpublished paper, Convention of the Leadership Conference of Women Religious, August 1989. For reflections on the influence of community and context on interpretation of texts, see: Regis Duffy, "Symbols of Abundance, Symbols of Need" in *Liturgy and Social Justice*, ed. by Mark Searle (Collegeville: The Liturgical Press, 1980); Segundo

express the commitment of members to one another and to common ideals, are essential to make community a living reality instead of a hoped-for ideal. The call to a simple life style, cross-generational and multi-cultural communication, global awareness, solidarity with the poor, and a contemplative approach to life mark the special qualities of the religiosity of authentic community living. In community life, these values are expressed in a public way which can be observed in the local church and civic community.

Community living is also needed for ongoing analysis of ministry experience. While social analysis is important, understanding the social, political, and economic relationships is not enough.[5] Through faith sharing, religious explore the quality of their relationships and global realities, imagine alternatives, and weigh them in light of the gospel.[6] Communities do not replace analysis with faith; rather, they allow faith to inform analysis so as to stretch the mind and heart to new possibilities.[7]

Community living, as a place where charism is interpreted, challenges the belief that there is a basic irreconcilability between people who do not share the same age, ethnic, class, racial, gender, or cultural background. In contrast, the gospel holds that reconciliation among people in community is not only possible, although difficult, but essential to hearing the word of God. As communities struggle to reconcile their ideological differences and move to a new way to interpret their lives today, they express the gospel which inspires them.

Contemplative mode of living

Through the help of community, one is more able to see both oneself and the other as human beings in touch with the Abso-

Galilea, *Following Jesus* (New York: Maryknoll, 1985); Sandra Schneiders, "The Effects of Women's Experience on Their Spirituality" in *Women's Spirituality*, ed. by Joann Wolski Conn (New York: Paulist Press, 1986).

5. See: Max Stackhouse, *Public Theology and Political Economy: Christian Stewardship in Modern Society* (Grand Rapids, Mich.: William B. Eerdmans, 1987).

6. Philip S. Keane, *Christian Ethics and the Imagination* (Ramsey: Paulist Press, 1984).

7. Johannes Metz discusses this point in his treatment of "narrative" in *Faith in History and Society, op. cit.*

lute, even amid the darkness of the contradictions of ministerial life. This contemplative way of living in the world marks the fourth moment in the living cycle of religious.[8]

On a practical level, contemplative insight can be a motivation for ministerial planning. Contemplation can lead religious to seek means to close the gap between what ought to be and what is, in new ways. Contemplative insight can also help to create a common vision which unites those who, at face value, may appear diverse and unconnectable. A community celebrates a contemplative way of living in public worship, where what appears to be ordinary is given its proper perspective as the locus of God's intervention. As a mysticism flowing from community living, the contemplative vision of its members can give congregational ministry its political and public thrust.[9]

The ongoing process

The four moments of ministry, community, reflection, and contemplation-in-action complete the cycle of living for a religious, but only for a moment. Soon the vision fades. Conflicts, changing relationships, and shifting needs plunge religious again into the first moment of ministerial reinvestment. On one level this happens daily; on another, at times of ministerial transition. As the cycle continues, religious experience their vocation unfolding through the support and challenge of community. While all Christians will share with the religious all phases of this cycle, it is the communal aspect which specifically marks a distinctive aspect of his or her vocation. Religious experience the liminality of life through prayer, ministry, nature, friendship, the arts, and personal gifts. However, unifying and giving a context for each is the experience of community.

While today there are a diversity of ways religious build community and participate in its formation, congregational life and local

8. See, for example: Thomas H. Green, *Darkness in the Marketplace* (Notre Dame: Ave Maria Press, 1981). John Veltri, *Orientations*, Vol. I. (Guelph, Ontario: Loyola House, 1983).

9. Gustavo Gutierrez, "Liberation, Theology and Proclamation," in Claude Geffre and G. Gutierrez, eds., *The Mystical and Political Dimension of Christian Faith* (New York: Herder and Herder, 1974) 57–77.

living centers are essential as visible signs of communal activity elsewhere. For those who are in mission and living alone, these centers can provide a base where they can share with those who profess their congregational vision. Local living centers can also be part of a network of "communities" which are not local living groups, but are formed around an interest in sharing in a congregational charism as an interpretative framework for lay ministry.

Characteristics of a community

Communities able to move beyond the present transitional phase of community life will be distinguished by three characteristics. They will be organic, participative, and discerning.

ORGANIC

Communities spring from mission. In contrast to groups formed around a special interest, the community gets its bonding power from a common mission to a local church. It is unusual for all members in a local community to share the same work, and it is not common today. However, communities and community members living in a specific area can develop a ministry outlook which links the individual ministries of members to a sense of communal charism and mission.

The concept of local church is a rich resource for the formation of religious community. Local church can be a parish-based group or a diocese or a geographical area.[10] Members who have ministries which are not under the auspices of a church group still minister to the local church, just as the universal church ministers to the world in ways not directly associated with formal religious institutions.

An organic relationship to a particular mission strengthens the bonds of community living, since community life is face-to-face living in mission, not a life-style enclave separated from ordinary life. As members of other communities, religious build community, sharing in groups organic to ordinary life: parishes, neighbor-

---

10. Some of the richness of this sense of the Church is discussed in Robrecht Michiels, "The Self-Understanding of the Church after Vatican II," *Louvain Studies* 14 (1989) 83–107.

hoods, community networks, geographical areas, migrant groups, refugee camps, senior citizens' complexes, Indian reservations, housing developments, universities, hospitals, shelters. Each of these living communities has a life of its own in which the religious shares.

An organic community life differs from a community style based on a vague sense of spiritual community which has no reality in face-to-face living at some level. Religious can have an organic vision of community and still recognize that community involvement has its rhythms over a life cycle. At different moments of life, the opportunity, need, or desire for face-to-face living may differ. However, over the long term, the vocation of a religious is essentially communal and some type of organic community living forms a basis of this life style.

PARTICIPATIVE

Transformative communities feel the need for other communities, including the wider Church, for their survival and well being. This is a very difficult achievement today, as some religious feel alienated either from members of their own community or from the Church. However, the separation needed to work through an alienation is not a permanent stance in a transformative community. There is no long-term future for alienated groups living separately from one another today. In a transformative community, groups will move beyond healing and seek new ways to live corporately.

Communities express their participatory character through a communal global consciousness. In the last thirty years, religious have had a micro-ethical focus. Many have wrestled with inner psychological issues. The traditional struggle against inordinate attachments, acquisitive instincts, and accumulative tendencies has been extended to facing the weaknesses in one's own psychological structure. Religious have benefited from the focus on both of these dimensions of conversion.

These internal forces, however, also have an archetypical nature.[11] "Mammon" is not only within people. It is a cosmic power

_____

11. See, for example: the work of the Jungian analyst Marion Woodman, *Addiction to Perfection: The Still-Unravished Bride* (Toronto: Inner City

of principalities and powers which creates inequalities and injustices among human beings.[12] The battle against these forces has to be fought on the macro-ethical level of public policy, education, ecological consciousness, and economics. Most communities are aware that both personal and social conversion are important. However, transformative communities recognize the need of other communities to help them move from an inner focus to an outward one. Inappropriate withdrawal and separatism is a sign of inauthenticity.

DISCERNING

Discernment is the ability to know how God is acting in life and, consequently, how to measure decisions. Transformative communities discern; that is, they have the capacity to use many kinds of thinking and evaluation to meet the problems that confront them and the people with whom they walk. Transformative communities can use their heads *and* their hearts. They can face the challenges of the future without slipping into romantic isolationism or the irrelevancy of abstraction.

Transformative communities rely on good conceptual knowledge. Conceptual knowledge is knowledge about reality. At one level, it is knowledge of the major intellectual disciplines and the arts. At another, it is knowledge about rules, values, and strategies for right living that can be passed on from one generation to another. Possession of conceptual knowledge does not make communities act; rather, commitment is necessary. Acquiring knowledge, however, is a first step toward a focused response to today's reality.

Recent research has noted that religious communities underplay this aspect of life. In the last few decades, the hard intellectual work required to analyze reality has been replaced by a "workshop" approach to complicated issues.[13] Anti-intellectualism has grown in religious congregations as a reaction against the highly conceptual formation that some religious experienced. However, transformative communities—as they face serious decisions—are

Books, 1982); *The Pregnant Virgin: A Process of Psychological Transformation* (Toronto: Inner City Books, 1985); *The Ravaged Bridegroom* (Toronto: Inner City Books, 1988).

12. Aloysius Pieris, *Love Meets Wisdom, op. cit.*, 91.

13. This study is yet unpublished.

overcoming this tendency and reasserting their traditional grounding in a solid intellectual life.

Transformative communities also draw on evaluative knowledge as they discern. Conceptual and evaluative knowledge are similiar to right- and left-brain reasoning. In contrast to conceptual knowledge, evaluative knowledge is knowing the worth or value of a matter. This type of knowledge cannot be easily passed on through statements, formulas, or rules. Rather, it is learned through personal involvement and mutual witness.[14] One way transformative communities learn this type of discernment is by allowing those within their ministries to pose to the community new questions and allowing these questions to transform them.

Why is discernment so essential for communities of the future? Transformative communities sift the positive and negative aspects of the prevailing ideologies, or world views, of today. Without this critical ability, the pluralism of the culture and, subsequently, the pluralism among community members, makes community life impossible. There is no single consensus, which the culture provides, around which a community can form. In such a climate, the temptation to grab hold of some world view or movement and name it as the community center is strong.

However, no movement, whether it is feminism, ecological consciousness, new-age religion, or religious fundamentalism is strong enough to give a congregation identity. Without the careful discernment of societal movements and how they help or hinder the mission and life of the congregation, no real communal vision in tune with societal life is formed. Transformative communities use this type of discernment in their congregational planning and will encourage members to learn the skills necessary for this type of reflection.

The role of community in the living cycle of religious has certainly not been exhausted by these reflections. However, they are offered as a starting point for discussion of the place community holds in our lives. The four characteristics of a transformative community may be added to or critiqued. Maybe there are six characteristics or only two. Authors suggest paradigms for understanding our lives, but all of us create homes and environments where we

14. Timothy O'Connell, *Principles for a Catholic Morality, op. cit.*, chapter 5.

grow and prosper. The renewal of community life will not be accomplished through a neat theory or by a book. Rather, it will require the investment of loving men and women willing to continue
to search for new expressions of this special charism in the Church.
It is hoped these reflections contribute in some small way to this
journey.

CHAPTER FOURTEEN

The Cost of Being Church

Many people today do not share faith in Jesus Christ in the community of the Church. These people do profess a faith in God. However, they experience the Church as a block to faith. Among some religious this ambivalence toward the Church is also present. It is expressed in statements such as, "I can belong to my congregation, but I am not sure about the Catholic Church. It is sexist, elitist, bureaucratic, and generally lets me down."

Questioning the relationship between religious and the Church abounds in congregations today. We all know religious who are alienated from the Church. We listen to their stories of feeling caught between the official Church and people in the Church. As the Church struggles with problems of authority, sexuality, divorce and remarriage, priestly integrity and sexism, religious find themselves in the middle of this pain. We also recognize that some religious have an ambivalent relationship to the Church. They have had many new experiences. However, they have not found a way to integrate these new experiences into their identity in the Church. The question lingers among religious today over what it means to belong to the Church. Do I belong? What is my role?

Religious question relationship with the Church around practical and ministerial issues also. They ask whether ministry has to have anything to do with the Church. What bearing do the vows have on ministry? Could we do our ministry just as well without the vows and without the Church? How do we measure authentic ministry in our congregation? Do we minister anymore as a congregation? Who is the focus of our ministry? What do we hope to accomplish in ministry?

These questions have personal ramifications which no theory can address. They call for an informed faith response. Just as Jesus once asked the apostles, "Who do you say that I am?," religious today have to ask, "What is the Church for me, and for us as a community?" The search for a renewed faith in the Church, in face of the ambiguities of membership today, is unavoidable. One way religious enter into this search is by reflecting on the meaning of their ministry in the Church.

In this chapter we will ask three questions which concern the relationship between Church and ministry today. How does the Church see itself as minister? Is the Church necessary for ministry? What is the relationship between the Church and the ministry of the religious?

1. How Does the Church See Itself as Minister?

The many faces of the search for salvation

Many people hunger for the mystery which lies at the heart of the Church for meaning in their lives.[1] They search for wholeness or for salvation. While Christians recognize that the search for meaning is the search for salvation in the face of sin, there are many languages for expressing this search today.

We rarely call our human search, a search for salvation. We express this desire through other forms of its manifestation.[2] Individuals struggle for rebirth in the face of death, in a society of increasing medical technology and aging. They hunger for justice before injustice, and religious experience, for them, centers in working for social change or overcoming the alienation unjust structures have put on them.

Others seek wholeness before disease in its physical and psychic forms. Much of their energy is spent trying to understand their experience and overcome limitations. Some unconsciously hunger for meaning instead of chaos. They go from one meaning system

1. The introduction to the Bishop's Economic Pastoral (*op. cit.*) is a good example of the type of needs witnessed in ministry today.
2. Roger Haight, "Salvation in Liberation Theology" *The Ecumenist*, (Jan–Feb., 1988) 17–21.

to another to order their lives and learn new life skills. Many ministries in religious congregations touch some form of this search for salvation.

As they participate in these ministries, religious ask what is the Church, in the face of these questions that people pose. Who and what is included within the scope of the care of the Church? Some religious feel that the people they meet in ministry are beyond the care of the Church. Their ecclesiology and their ministry experience is in tension.

A shift in the self-understanding of the Church

Religious experience a gap between their ministry experience and the image of the Church that they have formed through the years. Changes in theology since the Vatican Council have widened this gap for some. Vatican I stated that outside the Church there is no salvation.[3] This narrowed quite a bit the scope of the ministry of the Church. It was principally sacramental and directed toward Catholics. When religious engaged in this type of ministry, they saw their ministry as centered in the Church. When they did not, relationship to the Church was unclear.

Vatican II modified the Vatican I view. It stated that the grace of Christ's redemption is not found only in the Roman Catholic Church; rather, it subsists in it or resides in it in a unique way.[4] Vatican II's understanding of the Church did not stress a triumphal Church, rather a Church which relies on the Spirit for its holiness. The deepest identity of the Church is not her achievement, rather the gift of the Spirit within her.[5] The Council reminded us that the life of the Spirit exists in the world also, not just in the Church.

3. Avery Dulles, *The Catholicity of the Church* (January–February, 1988) (Oxford: Clarendon Press, 1985) 15–21.

4. *Lumen gentium* 8. "This Church, constituted and organized in the world as a society, subsists in the Catholic Church, which is governed by the successor of Peter and by the bishops in union with that successor, although many elements of sanctification and of truth can be found outside her visible structure." *The Documents of Vatican II*, ed. by Walter M. Abbott (New York: Herder and Herder, 1966).

5. *Ibid.*, 7.

Vatican II stressed a Church in mission. Because of God's gift, the Church has the grace to recognize the Spirit in other places.[6] The fullness of the grace of Christ's redemption is found not only in the Roman Catholic Church, but in the Church of Christ, meaning the communion of all who believe. The Church of Vatican II is in mission with all people of good will.

The Church of Vatican II recognized that grace existed beyond its boundaries. The grace of Christ operates in all people of good will, calling them to salvation and disposing them to accept the gospel if and when they hear it proclaimed in a manner in which they can hear it.[7] The Vatican II definition of the Church is much broader than Vatican I; consequently, the Church's understanding of its ministry is also expanded. Religious today need to integrate Vatican II understandings of the Church with their ministry experience.

All the concerns and struggles of the human community are appropriate foci for the ministry of the Church.[8] While most religious know the theology of Vatican II, this theology does not always penetrate deeper attitudes toward the Church. Often these attitudes come, not from theology but from disappointment and conflict in ministry.

However, if religious live in a state of alienation from the Church, much is lost. Along with the Church, in their ministry, religious are a sign there is meaning and direction to life.[9] Acting on behalf of the Church, religious extend its ministry to new places. In nonsacramental works, with those who are not Church members, religious are sometimes the first to minister in the name of the Church. Despite these facts, the question remains among some religious today whether the Church is necessary for the ministry of religious.

6. Avery Dulles, "Authority and Conscience" in *Readings in Moral Theology No. 6: Dissent in the Church*, ed. by Charles E. Curran and Richard A. McCormick, S.J. (New York: Paulist Press, 1988) 100–101. See also: *Gaudium et Spes*, art. 40.

7. Avery Dulles, *The Catholicity of the Church*, 21–22. See also: *Lumen gentium*, arts. 8, 9, 13, 16–17.

8. *Gaudium et Spes*, art. 4. *The Documents of Vatican II*, ed. by Walter M. Abbott (New York: Herder and Herder, 1966).

9. Gustavo Gutierrez, *A Theology of Liberation, op. cit.*, 101–131.

2. Is the Church Necessary for Ministry?

Since the Enlightenment, people have been wary about placing any confidence in the Church as a place where they could find God and find help with their life issues. Some religious are in a similar place of alienation. In the past, people have placed their confidence in pure reason or science instead of the Church. Philosophy or science became the point of contact with what was mysterious or expanding in their lives. People gave up religion or the practices associated with a community of belief. They believed virtue was sufficient for a good life and could be practiced independently of any religious group.[10]

Others rejected the hierarchical Church which developed after the Reformation. They saw Church as legalistic, giving divine authority to human ecclesiastical regulations and institutions. People became suspicious of rules and turned to Scripture alone for ethical direction. They gave up sacramental practice and a community of belief. They professed what they called a purely biblical religion which seemed not to have the pitfalls of organized religion.[11] We see evidence of this attitude in some forms of fundamentalism today.

Some groups had trouble with changes in the Church. They claimed that the real Church is the early Church and that the structures and changes which followed are inauthentic, or they canonized the present and future of the Church and depreciated the past.[12] A contemporary reaction in the Church is the post-Christian position. For these people, the period of institutional Christianity is coming to an end and is about to be superceded by an age of the Spirit, in which every individual will be guided interiorly without the need of external authority.[13] Religion is reduced to the inner feelings of an individual before God, without the need of a Church structure.[14]

---

10. This is the position of the rationalists. Patrick Granfield, "The Church as *Societas Perfectae* in the Schemata of Vatican I" *Church History* 46 (1979) 436.

11. Avery Dulles, *The Catholicity of the Church*, 16–18.

12. *Ibid.*, 98.

13. *Ibid.*, 99.

14. Robert Bellah, *Habits of the Heart, op. cit.,* 233–234, 245–246.

A final tendency is another extreme. Instead of rejection of the Church, some claim the Church has no weaknesses at all. People give to the human structures of the Church a divine quality which exaggerates the mystery inherent in it. This tendency was fostered by the catechesis surrounding the Church as the *perfect society*. The Church understood itself in this way after the Reformation until Vatican II.[15] Apologetic in tone, the image of the Church as a perfect society was an attempt to meet the real or imagined threats to the Church during these turbulent times.[16]

Against those who pointed out the failures of the Church and said it was irrelevant, the Church counterattacked that it was set apart from the vicissitudes of other groups. It was a perfect juridical society of believers instituted by Christ with a papal and episcopal hierarchy. The mystery of the Church and its human presence got confused. The institutional dimension of the Church was overemphasized. In order to strengthen the image of the Church, the Church was compared to a state, and called a juridical society.

Emphasizing the immutability, indefectibility, and visibility of the Church, and seeing it as an institution like a state, created a lack of balance in people's minds between the Church as a juridical reality and the Church as the community who believes in Jesus Christ. The ramifications of this imbalance are still felt today as religious chafe at canonical language and the institutional dimension of the Church. This attitude in part also generates the question whether the Church is necessary for ministry.

If religious surveyed their congregations, they would find that all of the historical attitudes toward the Church which we discussed above exist in their communities. Many are upset with an overinstitutionalized Church. For others, the Church is the perfect society. However, most religious have a conscious or unconscious sense that the Church is both an institution and a mystery. The Church is more than some vague spiritual union. However, to undo the imbalance created by recent Church history, the Church of the fu-

15. Peter Canisius and Robert Bellarmine began to define the Church primarily in institutional terms, putting the accent on the divinely established hierarchy. For a discussion, see: Richard P. McBrien, *The Remaking of the Church* (New York: Harper & Row, 1973) especially 5, 47, 76, 121, 122.

16. Granfield, "Church as *Societas Perfecta*," 445 and the following.

ture needs to be an institution in which charism and juridical identity are each given a more balanced role.

For many religious, difficulties with the institution of the Church stems from too many experiences of its institutional and distant face, rather than its dynamic and charismatic face. When religious do some self-examination, they also find that, at times, they contribute to their own alienation. However, to answer the question of whether we need the Church to minister, religious have to reconnect with a healthy sense of the Church, rather than one focused solely on its shortcomings and weaknesses.

Taking a place in the Church

The Church is not merely a human organization concerned with God as an object. If it were, the question whether to leave the Church or not could be resolved by measuring whether it was effective in being a group concerned and interested in God. If the Church was effective, religious would stay; if not, they would leave. It isn't this simple.

Christians believe that Jesus Christ is the one who acts in the ministry of the Church.[17] All ministry in the Church is a continuation of the ministry of Jesus Christ. Through baptism and confirmation, we take on Jesus' life as the center of our own and receive the Spirit of Jesus to act in the manner of his life style within the community of believers and before the world.[18] It is difficult for religious to work through their alienation today without this context of belief.

One religious put it this way. "For some years I was angry at the Church; then one day I realized that without the Church I would have never known Jesus. Somehow that insight put my anger in perspective, and I was able to move past it." Experience in the Church today can be rough. Fidelity to it demands a creativity and asceticism which is challenging. The easiest solution, in such a time of transition, is to walk away. However, no experience of alienation is resolved without the bottom line of faith. This reality leads

17. Karl Adam, *The Spirit of Catholicism* (New York: The Macmillan Company, 1931) 15.

18. Mary Catherine Hilkert, "Women Preaching the Gospel," *Theology Digest* 33:4 (Winter, 1986) 423–440.

us to our final question of the relationship of religious to the Church.

3. What is the Relationship between the Church and the Ministry of the Religious?

For the religious as minister, relationship to the Church takes on another level of understanding. Religious life does not make sense without a relationship to Jesus Christ any more than the Church makes sense without faith in its mystery, or one's congregation makes sense without faith in its charism. Belief that one comes to know Jesus Christ in a unique way through the community of the Church has an essential bearing on the ministry of religious.

In religious life, the experience of God above all else gives energy for the integration of the person.[19] While every encounter with God has many dimensions to it—physical, psychological, biological, social, political, and cultural—it is the ability of all human experience to mediate the experience of God which engages the religious.[20] The essential meaning of religious life involves a response to the experience of God in such a manner that one's entire life is restructured and redirected.[21]

This response to an experience of God is total. As a vocation, religious life involves all spheres of human experience and is oriented toward meaningful relationships with God and other human beings over an entire life cycle.[22] The vows symbolize that response to God does not just involve the mind and will but extends to the whole person. Response to God and God's people brings about a transformation and an enlivening of the entire person.[23]

19. Alejandra Cussianovich, *Religious Life and the Poor* (New York: Orbis Books, 1975) 21–43.

20. William A. Barry, "Interpretation of Experiences Reveals Beliefs" *Human Development*, Vol. 9, No. 2 (Summer, 1988) 20.

21. Leonardo Boff, *God's Witnesses in the Heart of the World*, trans. and ed. by Robert Fath (Chicago: Claret Center for Resources in Spirituality, 1981) 69.

22. Helen Flaherty, "Religious Life in the U.S.—A Guess at the Future" in *Religious Life in the U.S. Church: The Dialogue*, ed. by Robert Daly *et. al.* (New York: Paulist Press, 1984) 303.

23. Sandra M. Schneiders, *New Wineskins: Re-imaging Religious Life Today* (New York: Paulist Press, 1986) 61ff.

The ministry of a religious reflects the heart of his or her life—relationship with God. As Jesus' words and deeds reflected who he was, so the ministry of a religious reflects that belief in God is at the center of his or her life-style. The witness of religious life is to put people in contact with God and God's action in their lives.[24]

God's action is manifested in the many ways people hunger for wholeness or salvation: liberation from sin, rebirth before death in its many forms, justice before injustice, wholeness before disease. Religious life, however, is a life of clarity. Religious witness that in these diverse experiences of the search for life, stands the presence of God. Some authors see religious witness as a parable rather than an essay.[25] Regardless of how one pictures religious life, religious witness to the presence of God in the midst of all of life's journeys.

Religious experience growth in their vocation through an urgency to love through ministry, and in their later years, through the ministerial dimension of their prayer. However, many people experience an urgency to help people and to pray for them. A person does not need to be a religious to do either. Religious vows, however, express the motivation behind the ministerial urgency of religious and the manner in which they carry it out.[26]

Discipleship according to the vows marks an authentic ministry for religious. As they discern and respond to real need, they develop in their intimacy with Jesus Christ. Intimacy with Jesus Christ and ministry are inseparable for a religious.[27] Jesus Christ

24. Leonardo Boff, *God's Witnesses in the Heart of the World*, 84.

25. For a description of clarity as a gift of the Holy Spirit, see: Jules J. Toner, S.J. *A Commentary on Saint Ignatius' Rules for the Discernment of Spirits* (St. Louis: The Institute of Jesuit Sources, 1962) 69ff. See also: John M. Lozano, *Life as Parable: Reinterpreting Religious Life* (New York: Paulist Press, 1986) 38ff. Sandra M. Schneiders, *New Wineskins*, 217. Leonardo Boff, *God's Witnesses in the Heart of the World*, 85ff.

26. See: n. 9, chapter 9.

27. Alejandra Cussianovich, *Religious Life and the Poor*, 40ff. Here, the balance between the sense of the Absolute which flows from intimacy with Jesus Christ and a concrete analysis of the real demands of people of our times with an option for the poor is stressed.

is the primary personal center in whom all conversion and growth in the life of a religious finds wholeness.[28]

What is the relationship of the Church to the ministry of the religious? Religious do not practice a personal mysticism where religion is reduced to their inner feelings before God. Rather, in baptism, the communal and ecclesial nature of religious life is made evident. We only enter into covenant with God by becoming members of the covenant community, the Church.

The vows also plunge the religious into a broader community of covenant. The community, not just the individuals who are its members, is a covenant partner of God, also.[29] Baptism and religious vows set the stage for a life of ministry where the religious is always operating out of the interlocking circles of congregation and the Church.

Religious profession in a congregation is also a statement about ministry. Religious state that they have heard the promise of God through the ministry of others in the community and the Church, and are willing to stake their life and future on God's fidelity. They trust that through their congregation and the Church, they will receive the necessary help to be faithful. In face of all the unknowns at the moment of profession, making vows connotes that knowledge of Jesus Christ acting in one's own life will be inseparably linked to the Church.

Belief does not take away the problems of membership and fidelity in the Church today. It does not take away the need to critique the Church or to prod it to be faithful to its call to the Kingdom. But if it is a belief, it forms a value or center which is directive of action. As any relationship, relationship with the Church cannot grow without faith and trust.

As transformative communities reflect on their relationship with the Church, they do not seek a dependence on the Church but an interdependence with it. They reflect their covenant with God through thinking with the Church as it addresses human and global needs. They also contribute to the life of the Church through ac-

28. For a description of the multifaceted dimensions of conversion, see: Donal Dorr, *Spirituality and Justice* (New York: Orbis Books, 1984) 8–18.

29. Thomas Clarke, "Jesuit Commitment—Fraternal Covenant?" in *Studies in the Spirituality of the Jesuits, op. cit.*, 79.

tive membership in it, creative development of its renewal, and healthy criticism when necessary.

Thinking it over

In the midst of the immediacy of the current situation, congregations need to discern the value which membership in the Church holds out to them in meeting the needs of the present. Relationship to the Church has bearing on several areas of the ministry for religious. Because we are members of the Church, our vow of obedience is linked to the mission of the Church community. We are called to be apostolically mobile. The call to apostolic mobility conflicts with the stress of finding work at all for some religious. However, relationship to the Church gives the ministry of religious a value orientation. It makes job security and comfort-in-routine, lesser values than response to Church needs. Religious life is structured so that risks can be taken to promote the mission of the Church.

Second, relationship to the Church requires religious to be willing to share with the community of the Church and to act out their story as they minister. This, too, can be a source of conflict. The easiest roles in the Church today are either Church basher and reactionary, or someone who deals with all new questions with denial and denunciation. When religious reclaim their relationship to the Church, they keep alive the memory of God's ways by a sense of worship and a sacramental life which are both integral to ministry.

Religious learn about faith through the community of the Church. It is this logic which grounds their willingness to risk inserting themselves into ministry today. The faith of others in the Church opens them to the demands of conversion. It strengthens their sense of solidarity and collaboration with those with whom they journey. The reason why religious minister is because in their hearts they are—as were their founders and foundresses—ecclesial men and women. Amid the pain and challenge of carrying the cross of the Church today, this awareness is essential to their identity as religious in ministry.

CHAPTER FIFTEEN

Charism and New Partnerships

Charism gives religious congregations their basic identity.[1] Founders and foundresses discovered that certain reoccurring aspects of the mystery of God integrated diverse life experiences for them. If we put together the pieces of their spirituality, we meet the special character of their faith and of the charism of the groups which they founded.[2]

This experience of God expressed itself in varied choices: to serve the poor, to evangelize through health care or education, not to be cloistered but to make ministry an integrating focus in spirituality, to be international rather than diocesan. Their faith caused them to build bridges between their experience of God and the problems of their day.[3] Charism is not simply their special faith. It also involves the way they structured congregational life so that others would be able to share that same experience of God. Congregations today face the same challenge as these great people—to refound their orders through this same process.

1. Jean Marie Renfro, S.S.S., "Religious Charism: Definition, Rediscovery and Implications," *Review for Religious*, Vol. 45, No. 4 (July/August, 1986), 528.

2. A paradigm for approaching a congregation's spirituality in terms of the faith of the founder or foundress is found in Jon Sobrino, "The Faith of Jesus" in *Christology at the Crossroads* (New York: Orbis Books, 1970) 79–145.

3. In the deepest sense of the term this is called an ideology, a necessary system of means and ends. See: Carl Starkloff, "Ideology and Mission Spirituality" *Review for Religious* Vol. 45, No. 4 (July/August 1986) 554–566.

Handing on charism today

A key question for congregations today is how to hand on their charism. Every charism took hold because it named an effective connection between a deep experience of faith and a cry of the age.[4] The actual work of the new order communicated a message of God's redemption because it met an important need of that time. Without this marriage between spiritual insight and felt need, no charism would have attracted followers.

A problem in handing on charism today is the difficulty in reconnecting a charism, which was once linked to a single work, with the variety of ministries now found in many congregations. During renewal, many communities put less emphasis on institutions. They focused on meeting new needs and on helping their members find and develop personal gifts and talents for ministry. This has resulted in a more enlivened sense of connection between work and life among religious.

When congregations had a single ministry, handing on charism was seen as closely linked to supporting this particular work. Most congregations cannot do this anymore. While some congregations retain many members in a major, formal ministry, some of their members are also involved in other actions for social change, educative and health care ministry, and pastoral work.

Institutional centers of traditional ministries are still important. These centers can be a sign or sacrament of a congregational charism which can give solidity and witness to those in new ministries and endeavors. Those in new situations can challenge these institutional centers to incorporate their new learnings and keep relevant. The institutionalization of charism need not be limited to long-established centers of ministry. New needs may also require that the investment represented by these large endeavors be invested elsewhere. The question today is in what new places this integral incarnation of charism needs to be carried out.

To make charism more visible today, however, these new abilities and ministries need to be reintegrated into more communal projects that can make an impact on a local area. Without this more-corporate meeting of needs—whether by ministry teams doing

4. Bernard J. Lee, S.M., ''A Socio-Historical Theology of Charism,'' *Review for Religious*, Vol. 48, No. 1 (January/February 1989) 124–135.

different works, or collaborative efforts among congregations with complementary charisms—handing on charism will be difficult because it will be imperceptible.

Key also to handing on charism is attention to change in the social context . Movement theologically from the time of the inception of many religious congregations has been toward a gradual embrace of the world as the place for personal and spiritual development. This gives rise to a need for a type of evangelization which is focused on how to be whole in society rather than through withdrawing from the society.

In a society where choice is possible for many, eliciting partnership in ministry has to appeal to this freedom. Both new members and associates seek to answer these questions: "What will I do with the freedom which I find in my life? What type of contribution can I make?" Congregations who, through concrete projects, can offer viable alternatives to nihilism, determinism, and individualism as the only responses to modern problems will attract people to join with them in ministry, and thus hand on their charism.

Characteristic relationship to the Church

Most congregations have either a local or national focus or an international thrust to their self-understanding. Regardless of their tradition, a healthy link between the local and global Church is needed for communicating charism today. Central to either self-understanding is the reality of the perennial expansiveness of the grace of God. All charisms reflect the awareness that God's Spirit shows up in new places.[5] However, in today's Church, it is often in linking global and local Churches that this newness is in evidence.

It is also commonplace in the history of the Church that new evidences of grace and life are opposed by massive obstacles. Interpretation of charisms today has to take this into account. Congregations need to relate their own story to the issues facing the people of the world and the Church who are on pilgrimage to a more human life. To do this, they must do the social analysis neces-

5. This approach to religious life and its openness to the unexpected is developed in Johannes B. Metz, *Followers of Christ*, trans. Thomas Linton (New York: Paulist Press, 1978).

sary to reinterpret their story in terms of the real stories of the suffering of the world. The concerns of women, the support of Hispanic life in the Church and society, and the fight against racism and poverty seem to be major centers of this struggle in the United States today.

Focus on comparable world issues in light of charism naturally links the global and the local life of the Church. New crises arising in health care, ecology, war and peace, the international debt, North-South inequalities, and the impact of Asia and Africa on world consciousness are vital areas where congregations can re-articulate the relevance of their charism and through it insure its transmission.

A posture toward the poor

For many founders and foundresses, the poor were poor children and poor families. Today there are new categories for understanding the poor which are essential for the translation of charism. Among them, it seems four are especially relevant. First, there are poor nations not just poor people.[6] The interpretation of charism today has to address underdeveloped nations and how their needs are elements in a congregation's focus in mission.

Second, the poor are a social class, not just individuals. Since their life experience is tied to their place in society, not just to their personal character and achievements, the interpretation of charism has to be based on a social analysis which takes this into account. Priority should be given to ministries which have the potential for enabling the upward mobility of the poor not just caring for their immediate needs.[7]

Thirdly, the poor are not only economically poor but also politically marginated.[8] Interpretation of charism in light of the needs

6. Donal Dorr, *Option for the Poor: A Hundred Years of Vatican Social Teaching* (New York: Orbis Books, 1983) 139ff.

7. See: Francis Schussler Fiorenza, "Political Theology and Liberation: an inquiry into their fundamental meaning," in T. McFadden. *Liberation, Freedom and Revolution* (New York: Seabury Press, 1975) 17.

8. Donal Dorr, *Option for the Poor*, 222. Here Dorr discusses the humanistic criterion of John Paul II for evaluating various political and economic sys-

of the poor should take into consideration ministry initiatives which enable them to achieve social and political power, not just economic stability. Fourthly, option for the poor theologically points to the fact that the Spirit manifests itself in the poor. This makes them structural channels for finding the truth of the Church and the direction and content of its mission today.[9] Hence, service to the poor is not only an aspect of the work of many congregations but the ministry which keeps them close to the direction and content of the interpretation of their charism.

The call for a new corporateness

Many religious today sense that a new corporateness is needed to translate the vision of their charism into some visible form. They know this form cannot simply be a new uniformity in ministry. Charism cannot be reduced to only one concrete expression. On the other hand, charism withers without a visible life style to embody it. The paradox of charism is that it is not just a vision but a life that takes visible form.

The question before religious congregations is what direction does their charism give them in ministry as they move toward the beginning of the next millennium? Empirical evidence indicates that collaboration will likely be one of the main vehicles by which religious express their charism.[10] If this is true, collaboration can not mean just a vague sense of spiritual union among loosely organized priests, religious, and lay ministers. Rather, collaboration can be a new way of organizing and understanding mission.

tems in *Redemptor Hominis.* ". . . the fundamental criterion for comparing social, economic and political systems . . . must be . . . the humanistic criterion, namely, the measure in which each system is really capable of reducing, restraining and eliminating as far as possible the various forms of exploitation of man and of ensuring for him through work, not only the just distribution of the indispensible material goods, but also a participation, in keeping with his dignity, in the whole process of production and in the social life that grows up around that process."

9. Jon Sobrino, *The True Church and the Poor, op. cit.,* 95.

10. Helen Flaherty, "Religious Life in the U.S.—A Guess at the Future," 301.

Collaboration as another ministry model

For the greater part of this century, religious understood themselves in ministry through a highly institutionalized model. Later, to meet new needs, many congregations implemented a choice-of-ministry approach to missioning. This reflected a more personalized model. At this stage, some groups are feeling the gaps created by some of these changes and are asking for new institutions to assist them with a greater sense of identity and support in ministry.

When the words "institution" or "structure" arise in conversation, often someone thinks of many rules and policies and the discussion stops with a polite but firm, "No thanks." However, the new image of institution which can bridge the tension between the extremes of too much personalism and over-institutionalization is one where rules and charism are held in better balance.[11] It should be structured in order to experience and see things differently, life before death.[12] Collaboration will be a key element of this model.

In theological language, the future is not "institution" as in "Church," the perfect society where mainly the stability of the Church is stressed. Rather, the future for religious congregations may be characterized more by the work of the Spirit which is bonding. They are called to bring the substance and stability of the center of the Church—Jesus Christ—into consciousness and effectiveness in the world.[13]

Making better connections

The institutional component of ministry in the future has to be reshaped not only to assist congregations with a greater sense of identity but also in order to meet new needs. People need to make connections between God and life. Ministers need to make a connection between the Church and the world. Congregations

11. Donald L. Gelpi, "The Church: Sacramental and Charismatic, Avoiding False Dichotomies," *Church* (Spring, 1987) 19–24.

12. Juan Luis Segundo, *Historia y Actualidad: Sinopticos y Pablo* (Madrid: Cristianidad, 1982) 503. See this work also as: *The Humanistic Christology of Paul* (New York: Orbis, 1987).

13. Avery Dulles, *The Catholicity of the Church*, 44ff.

need to make connections between their communities and the rapidly changing Church and society.

The connections made for ministry have to be more than inspirational; they must also be geared toward a wise use of personal and financial resources for ministry. Congregations have to be concerned with achieving financial stability and having real people to do the work they envision. In the future, the model of ministry does not seem to be the institutionalization of the Church, rather its reintegration. This suggests that the future of ministry in religious congregations is not over, only different.

This new institutional component of ministry, which includes greater collaboration, will be grounded in a different theological motif. Instead of an institutional focus which emphasizes incarnation—making stable and permanent images of Christ's redemptive work among people—this new model emphasizes the work of the Spirit—bonding people to the Church and the Church to the world. This is the style of collaboration rather than institutionalization. A brief look into the work of the Spirit and the style of ministry which could flow from it can illustrate this new grounding.

Holy Spirit and a new style of ministry

The Holy Spirit is the feminine principle in the Trinity who is the bond of love between the Father and the Son, and who unites the Word to Jesus' humanity.[14] A ministry of collaboration is primarily one of bonding. As a style of ministry, it seeks to bond people to one another and the Church, and to their deepest selves, freeing them for growth according to their most urgent personal and social needs. It seeks to create unity among greater diversity without violating people as unique persons.

It is important to note that the work of the Holy Spirit is not to add to the revelation of Jesus Christ. Rather, the Spirit assists people to understand the words of Jesus from the inside, to lay hold of these words in the light of faith and discover all their historical possibilities and richness. A ministry of collaboration is one com-

14. *Ad Gentes*, 4. In *The Documents of Vatican II*, ed. by Walter M. Abbott (New York: Herder and Herder, 1966). See also: Juan Luis Segundo, *Our Idea of God* (New York: Orbis Books, 1973) 33.

mitted to dialogue among religious themselves, with colleagues, and with people who do not speak their religious or cultural language. Through this dialogue, they can better grasp the Word and draw out its meaning for transformative action in the world.

The work of the Spirit is also one of presence. The Spirit is the continuing presence who illumines and preserves the truth of God's covenant with men and women in spite of change and the inherent obscurity of their lives. When and where the values of Jesus are most obscure, this sustained presence is most needed.[15] Through various collaborative efforts, a congregation can provide this presence and extend its potential for it through others. Committed presence by a congregation through its collaborative efforts can communicate hope in situations of struggle, strengthening those who want to believe that the values of Jesus are worth their effort. It makes the work of the Spirit concrete before the fear of the disintegration of Church presence felt by many today.

Ramifications on ministry

What will be the ramifications of a ministry style of bonding, dialogue, and committed presence? First, the work of collaboration is not aimed primarily at membership. Its focus is to link people to the Church and the Church to the world. Full membership in a religious congregation, through vows, only flows from interest in this project and is not integral to it.

Second, collaboration should be aimed toward expressing the meaning of God's activity in the world in a new way, not necessarily at creating some former model. This has special meaning for those struggling with the creation of new associations and federations of existing religious communities. A collaborative attitude also supports increased internal collaboration among congregations or those who share a common inspiration at the national and international level.

Lastly, a collaborative style of ministry has as a priority the enablement of continued discernment and action for the development of the work of the Church. Congregational presence in col-

15. Josef Pieper, *The Four Cardinal Virtues* (Notre Dame: University of Notre Dame Press, 1966) 128.

laborative efforts needs to be discerned so it is consistent with its respective charism. Groups cannot collaborate with everything and everyone in a formal manner; rather, they need to create some priorities around which they will network. This new style of collaboration also has to allow the Spirit to transform our hearts. I would like to comment briefly on this last idea.

Quality of collaborative relationships

Traditionally, religious life has been understood as a higher calling in the Church. After Vatican II, there was more affirmation of the secular call of the Christian life and less emphasis on the distinctive call of the religious life.[16] When religious identity is unclear, there can be the tendency simply to deny it has an identity in the Church. Or there can be a drive to reinforce its identity by maintaining dominative relationships and structures to keep a former inequality permanent. Since much of what has been said in these chapters addresses the first concern, in the next few pages I would like to address the second.

In informal ways, people in ministry across congregations have been engaged in collaboration for years. However, in a formal way they are just beginning new, organized efforts around collaboration. It seems important at this time to look at the relationship between domination and identity as it could affect this new effort.

Jean Miller, in her book *Toward a New Psychology of Women*, indicates that in a society aiming to keep inequality permanent, the following things occur: 1) the dominant labels the subordinate as inferior; 2) the dominant assigns to the subordinate the unpleasant tasks while keeping the preferred tasks for itself; 3) the dominant states further that the subordinate is unable to perform the preferred tasks; and 4) the dominant determines what is "normal" for the situation.[17]

It seems imperative that new efforts toward collaboration be structured in a manner which is sensitive to issues of domination.

16. Bonaventure Kloppenburg, *Ecclesiology of Vatican II* (Chicago: Franciscan Herald Press, 1974) 294–308.

17. Discussed in Mary Sheehan and Barbara Wheeley, "Psychological Aspects of a Search for Truth" in *Human Development*, Vol. 9, No. 2 (Summer, 1988) 13–16.

What complicates this venture is that there are religious on both sides of this fence. In some collaborative relationships, especially in Church structures, religious can experience themselves as the dominated. However, as agents of collaboration they can become the dominator. In addition, there are other factors which enter into man-woman ministry relationships in the Church. Tensions surrounding gender are probably some of the most critical in the Church today.

This situation has bearing on style of ministry, not only for individuals but also for congregations in ministry. People coming to religious congregations for partnership relationships are adult Christians who are members of a larger movement in the Church, that is, of ecclesial maturity. They bring gifts to the work of a congregation, but they also bring anger, autonomy, and a lot of experience. This will contribute to struggles which congregations are already wrestling with within themselves—difference of opinion, expectations of adult relationships, and needs for self direction. If religious and their congregations are willing to let go of past images of ministry, they will get involved in this maturing Church and truly collaborate in its new life. They will require the Church to respond to them in a manner which is consistent with its potential and be patient enough to build constructive relationships themselves.

Belief in the substance of a congregational charism as it faces new challenges affirms the relevancy of religious life. Lay ministry today is coming to the same conclusions. Many lay ministers are in need of some institution to support them in the spiritual and ministerial development they need over the long term. These people are not looking for a juridical structure nor a pseudo-marriage but a movement of bonding where their incipient actions in the new Church can find a place of focus, criteria for measuring and nurturing of community. A ministry-styled bonding, dialogue, and committed presence on the part of religious congregations may be the ground for a new partnership with these new companions in the living out of charism today.

Vowed membership

We have suggested that a theological understanding of ministry is related to an understanding of the Church. A model of the

Church based on Christ stresses how the Church is the permanent incarnation of Christ. However, a model of Church which is pneumatological or based on the Holy Spirit stresses how the fruits of Christ's redemption are continually present in new and unexpected ways.[18] Ecclesiologists remind us that a complete theology of the Church has to avoid both extremes and be Trinitarian. It must bring together a fruitful balance between stability and newness.[19]

What meaning does this have for religious congregations as they face the new challenge of increased collaboration? While the whole area of collaboration is so significant for the future, it is also important to keep in mind that the permanently vowed members of a congregation are the incarnation of its charism in an irreplaceable way. As the Word became flesh, by permanent commitment the vowed members of a religious community unite their whole life to its charism.

In this sense, the permanently vowed member may be to those who seek new forms of commitment in religious congregations what the Church is to its members. (Rahner says the Church as the visible form is what is already binding.)[20] Through the Church, members are to find visible helps and real power to discover the mystery of their persons which still remains hidden. In like manner, the continued unfolding of the meaning of vowed life in religious life today can also be a center through which new expressions can find stability and meaning. These new expressions, as those of others in previous centuries, will in some way support the investment and discernment which has always made religious life a commitment created by choice.

18. Michael Schmaus, *Dogma 4 The Church* (New York: Sheed and Ward, 1972) 84.

19. Avery Dulles, *The Catholicity of the Church*, 47. "The triune God who communicates self in the Incarnate Word and in the Holy Spirit, is the source and ground of catholicity."

20. Karl Rahner, *The Christian and the Future* (New York: Herder and Herder, 1967) 88.

A Commitment Created by Choice

What is involved in the choice of religious life in the Church today? In these pages we have sought to explore this question, both from the perspective of individuals who choose religious commitment, and those of congregations continuing in the process of renewal. The fact that religious life is a commitment created by choice seems even more evident as I complete the writing of this text.

To be a religious requires the choice to be countercultural, to step back from the definitions of autonomy held in society today. As an adult stance in the Church, it involves the choice to take up responsibility, by vow, for a better world. This calls for the choice to believe and invest—in the face of fewer members, increased financial concerns, and the crises of world poverty and skepticism today. Choice is needed to take the risks to continue to build creative ministry responses and collaborative efforts.

However, the choices made by religious in the last thirty years also have created the religious life experienced today. Juan Luis Segundo, a theological mentor whose works appear often in this text, has commented in his volume *Faith and Ideologies* that human freedom is such that choice, over a period of time, makes the reversal of those choices less and less possible. The use of freedom paradoxically limits its scope. One choice leads to another. Preferences begin to exclude other options as meaningful expressions of one's person.

This is true for religious congregations who have worked at renewal for the last thirty years. The risk involved in past choices makes it impossible to continue with things as they are, and remain healthy. To refuse to continue to change would bring a loss of meaning. It would require a rejection of the values which have guided congregations thus far. In order to continue to promote the dignity of persons, to focus on the needs of justice, and to contribute to the ongoing renewal of the Church, religious must move forward with their renewal.

The future of religious life will be a reversal of the renewal process thus far, only if religious stop choosing and hide—either in fear or in addictive relationships. The freedom religious have already gained has set their faces to brace the opposing winds of our times and create new possibilities in a world in transition. May these pages serve in some way to continue this marvelous journey, led by hearts who have known for many years how to choose and how to love.